Your Path to Purpose, Passion, and Peace

90 Days of Timeless Wisdom

Charles F. Stanley

Thomas Nelson
Since 1798

ZONDERVAN BOOKS

Your Path to Purpose, Passion, and Peace
© 2025 by Charles F. Stanley

Portions of this book adapted from *On Holy Ground* (ISBN: 9780785276623, © 1999).

Published by Zondervan, 3950 Sparks Drive SE, Suite 101, Grand Rapids, MI 49546, USA. Zondervan is a registered trademark of The Zondervan Corporation, L.L.C., a wholly owned subsidiary of HarperCollins Christian Publishing, Inc.

Requests for information should be addressed to customercare@harpercollins.com.

Zondervan titles may be purchased in bulk for educational, business, fundraising, or sales promotional use. For information, please email SpecialMarkets@Zondervan.com.

ISBN 9780310179214 (print)
ISBN 9780310179238 (audio)
ISBN 9780310179221 (ebook)

Unless otherwise noted, Scripture quotations in this publication are taken from the New King James Version®. Copyright © 1982 by Thomas Nelson. Used by permission. All rights reserved.

Scripture quotations noted New American Standard Bible®. Copyright © 1960, 1971, 1977, 1995 by The Lockman Foundation. Used by permission. All rights reserved. www.lockman.org.

Scripture quotations the Holy Bible, New International Version®, NIV®. Copyright © 1973, 1978, 1984, 2011 by Biblica, Inc.® Used by permission of Zondervan. All rights reserved worldwide. www.zondervan.com. The "NIV" and "New International Version" are trademarks registered in the United States Patent and Trademark Office by Biblica, Inc.®

Any internet addresses (websites, blogs, etc.) and telephone numbers in this book are offered as a resource. They are not intended in any way to be or imply an endorsement by Zondervan, nor does Zondervan vouch for the content of these sites and numbers for the life of this book.

All rights reserved. No portion of this book may be reproduced, stored in a retrieval system, or transmitted in any form or by any means—electronic, mechanical, photocopy, recording, scanning, or other—except for brief quotations in critical reviews or articles, without the prior written permission of the publisher.

Without limiting the exclusive rights of any author, contributor or the publisher of this publication, any unauthorized use of this publication to train generative artificial intelligence (AI) technologies is expressly prohibited. HarperCollins also exercise their rights under Article 4(3) of the Digital Single Market Directive 2019/790 and expressly reserve this publication from the text and data mining exception.

HarperCollins Publishers, Macken House, 39/40 Mayor Street Upper,
Dublin 1, D01 C9W8, Ireland (https://www.harpercollins.com)

Printed in the United States of America

25 26 27 28 29 LBC 5 4 3 2 1

Your Path to Purpose, Passion, and Peace

Introduction

No one wants an unfulfilling life. This is because God created you for an exciting spiritual journey that results in passion, purpose, and peace. But experiencing that kind of existence doesn't happen by accident. You cannot simply drift toward a fulfilling goal or an abundantly meaningful life. You must deliberately choose the path the Lord has mapped out for you and avoid pitfalls along the way.

This is where most of us wonder where we should even begin. This is why King David prayed, "Make me know Your ways, Lord; teach me Your paths. Lead me in Your truth and teach me, for You are the God of my salvation, for You I wait all the day" (Ps. 25:4–5 NASB). David understood that if he wanted to experience life at its best, the first step would be to seek God and follow Him. It would be wise for you to do so as well.

Therefore, for the next ninety days, *Your Path to Purpose, Passion, and Peace* will take you on a tour of the lives of several biblical saints who lived the kind of life you long for. They didn't get everything right, and they made plenty of mistakes along the way. But they learned from their missteps, stayed on the path, and pursued God's will for their lives. And they discovered as David did: "You will make known to me the path of life; in Your presence is fullness of joy; in Your right hand there are pleasures forever" (Ps. 16:11 NASB).

Naturally, before you start on a long journey, it's always a good idea to ensure you have all you need. The good news is that the Lord has already supplied you with everything essential for your spiritual journey. Second Peter 1:3 promises, "His divine power has granted to us everything pertaining to life and godliness, through the true knowledge of Him who called us by His own glory and excellence." Indeed, your passport—the blood of Jesus—was secured for you at Calvary. Your trustworthy Guide is the Holy Spirit, who will faithfully teach you as you go. And your guidebook—the Bible—has all the information you'll require along the way.

Nothing has been left out or forgotten; you are fully equipped for the adventure ahead and to embrace the life God has for you. Indeed, it's when you face your greatest needs—when you come to the end of your ability and feel the most lost—that you'll realize the absolute abundance and wisdom of His provision.

So set out with full confidence in the God who leads you. Trust Him and enjoy your journey.

DAY 1

The Pathway to Purpose

SCRIPTURE READING: Romans 4 KEY VERSE: Romans 4:18

Who, contrary to hope, in hope believed, so that he became the father of many nations, according to what was spoken, "So shall your descendants be."

Hannah Whitall Smith once wrote, "Sight is not faith, and hearing is not faith, neither is feeling faith; but believing when we neither see, hear, nor feel is faith ... Therefore, we must believe before we feel, and often against our feelings if we would honor God by our faith."[1]

When you read the account of Abram's life, you realize he was a man of faith. God asked him to do something most of us would find very difficult, and that was to leave his family and friends and go to an unfamiliar land.

Yet God's reassuring words lessened Abram's fear: "I will make you a great nation, and I will bless you, and make your name great; and so you shall be a blessing; and I will bless those who bless you" (Gen. 12:2–3 NASB).

Abram, or Abraham as he was later called by God, gave little thought to the fact that his name would be made great. The most important thing to him was the exercise of his faith through obedience.

Anytime God calls you to step out in faith, He will provide the reassurance you need to go forward by faith. Your only responsibility is to obey and follow Him. Abraham left everything simply because God said, "Go."

Goals for the Day

- Read Romans 4.
- Spend some time thinking about how Paul pointed to the life of Abraham to show that righteousness is credited through faith in God's promises, not through human effort.

Faith in Action

Write down Romans 4:3 or another passage that stood out to you in today's Bible reading. Is there a circumstance in your life where you need to exercise faith? Write down the details below.

_____

_____

_____

_____

_____

Heavenly Father, help me to believe, even when I do not see. Help me to trust when I do not hear Your voice. Give me the reassurance to step out in faith, even if it means letting go of something I care for dearly.

DAY 2

Defining Faith

SCRIPTURE READING: Psalm 24   KEY VERSE: Hebrews 11:1

*Faith is the substance of things hoped for,
the evidence of things not seen.*

What is faith? Faith is not a power or force that we can use to manipulate God to fit into our agenda. We're not that smart. Faith is not just confidence. It is not believing in yourself or feeling sure about the outcome of a certain event.

For example, you could visit the bleachers in a ball game, and each side would be confident its team would win. This is not biblical faith.

Faith is not confusing or complicated. It is not only the domain of educated people but is meant to be sought and applied by everyday folk in everyday life. Faith is not connected to circumstance. When all is well, we often think our faith is intact. But when foul conditions set in, what happens to our trust? As long as our faith is no deeper than our circumstance, we're set up for failure.

Authentic faith is simply this: God is who He says He is and will do what He says He will do. Our faith is in the person of Jesus Christ, in His character and attributes. It is completely trusting in the faithfulness of God to do what is right.

Goals for the Day

- Read Psalm 24.
- Make a timeline of your faith journey. What notable events have happened along the way? What would you like your faith to look like one year from now? Five years? Ten?

Faith in Action

Today's reading said, "Authentic faith is simply this: God is who He says He is and will do what He says He will do." How does this truth apply to your current circumstances?

_____

_____

_____

_____

_____

_____

_____

Dear Lord, give me authentic faith. I believe You are who You say You are, and You will do what You say You will do. My faith rests in Your faithfulness to do what is right in my life.

DAY 3

GETTING GOD'S PERSPECTIVE

SCRIPTURE READING: 2 Corinthians 4:7–12   KEY VERSE: 2 Corinthians 4:7

We have this treasure in earthen vessels, that the excellence of the power may be of God and not of us.

If you have ever flown in an airplane and peered out the window, you were probably enraptured with the view. In clear weather, you can see a vast landscape in one quick glance, allowing you to momentarily transcend the restrictive barriers of earthbound living.

It is but a minute portrait of how our omniscient, omnipotent God views the life of the believer. He sees all. He knows all. He is aware of every detail of your life from birth (even before you were conceived) until death.

Since God knows your future perfectly and how today's ordinary events fit into His plan, you can rely on Him every moment. The timeless principles of Scripture help you make wise decisions from God's viewpoint.

We are related to the all-seeing, all-knowing God who has given us resources to face life's challenges and obstacles from His perspective. We don't have to be limited by our own strength or wisdom.

We are hemmed in too often by our circumstances, unable to see through the fog of our finiteness. But if we seek God prayerfully and consistently, regularly digesting His Word, we can break through barriers with His insight.

Goals for the Day

- Read 2 Corinthians 4:7–12.
- Identify your biggest challenges in this season of your life. Ask God to help you confront these difficulties with biblical wisdom.

Faith in Action

Pick a passage from Scripture that speaks to the challenges you're facing. Write it below, on a notecard, or on your phone. Throughout the day, make it a point to pray the passage and ask God to apply the truths of Scripture to your current situation.

___

___

___

___

___

___

___

Father, You see all, know all, and are aware of every detail of my life. You have planned today's ordinary events to fit into Your long-range purpose for my life. As I travel through this day, help me break through barriers with Your insight.

DAY 4

The Call of Faith

SCRIPTURE READING: Genesis 12:1–9   KEY VERSE: Hebrews 10:23

Let us hold fast the confession of our hope without wavering, for He who promised is faithful.

Suppose you plan a wonderful surprise vacation for your family or friends. The big day finally comes. The car is loaded, everyone has taken care of all those last-minute details, and your tank is full of gas. Everyone piles in the car and fastens seat belts in anticipation.

Finally someone asks the fateful question, "Hey, where are we going?" And you say with great authority, "Well, I don't know exactly." After the bewildered looks and cries of dismay, probably the only one left in the car with you is the dog, and he isn't looking too certain either. People simply don't make big trips without knowing where they're going—unless God asks them to. And that is precisely what God asked of Abram and his family: "Go forth from your country, and from your relatives and from your father's house, to the land which I will show you; and I will make you a great nation, and I will bless you, and make your name great" (Gen. 12:1–2 NASB).

God gave them some very important information, but He did not hand them a road map. Why? He wanted them to trust Him for the journey. Abram did not know where they were headed, but he knew their future was blessed, more than he could conceive.

Goals for the Day

- Read Genesis 12:1–9.
- Spend a few moments in prayer asking God to reveal any areas you might be off track. Ask Him to direct your steps and guide you on His paths.

Faith in Action

Make a list of goals you'd like to accomplish. Do these goals bring glory to God? If you achieve your goals, will the outcome serve other people well?

_____

_____

_____

_____

_____

_____

_____

Lord, take me in Your direction. Help me learn to walk by faith. I know my future will be blessed, more than I can imagine. No travel plan is necessary for my journey—I need only You as my Guide.

DAY 5

Faith vs. Reason

SCRIPTURE READING: 1 Corinthians 1:18–29   KEY VERSE: Hebrews 10:38

Now the just shall live by faith; but if anyone draws back, my soul has no pleasure in him.

From humanity's point of view, not everything God does seems logical. There are times when we know what God is doing. Other times, all we can do is scratch our heads and think, *Lord, I don't understand, but I trust You because You know what is best.*

The basis of faith is not in knowing, but in trusting. Many people are tripped up in their faith at this point. When we insist on seeing and understanding where God is leading us before making a commitment to trust Him, we are living by human reason and not by faith.

Yet God calls each of us to live a life of faith. He said, "My righteous one shall live by faith" (Heb. 10:38 NASB). The author of Hebrews continued by writing: "Faith is the assurance of things hoped for, the conviction of things not seen" (Heb. 11:1 NASB).

Are you trusting God or reasoning your way through life? When you live by faith, things may not always turn out the way you think they will. God answers our prayers according to His will and timing. He knows some of what we ask for would lead only to heartache and grief. Therefore, He protects us by giving us the things He knows will bring blessing to us and honor to Himself.

Goals for the Day

- Read 1 Corinthians 1:18–29.
- Confess any areas you might be lacking in faith and ask God to give you faith that is pleasing to Him.

Faith in Action

Have you been waiting for a long time to see God work in a specific circumstance? If so, write down ways to rekindle your faith as you wait.

_____

_____

_____

_____

_____

_____

_____

_____

O God, there are times when I do not understand what You are doing. Let me learn to trust that You know what is best. Thank You for protecting me by answering my prayers according to Your will and perfect timing.

DAY 6

THREE PRINCIPLES OF SUCCESS

SCRIPTURE READING: Joshua 1:1–9   KEY VERSE: Joshua 1:9

Have I not commanded you? Be strong and of good courage; do not be afraid, nor be dismayed, for the LORD your God is with you wherever you go.

Jesus calmed the raging sea not so that the disciples could witness another miracle, but so that they might be caught up in the reality of His strength and personal care for them. Jesus allowed fear to captivate their hearts briefly so they could learn of Him. After the first few opening chapters of the book of Acts, we see His principles come to life in the lives of His followers. They found their strength in Jesus.

Joshua faced a similar situation as he prepared to lead Israel into the promised land. Chosen by God to complete the task, Joshua struggled with thoughts of fear and failure.

The angel of the Lord gave him three principles to keep him focused on the victory of God's strength: (1) meditate on the Word of God daily; (2) focus, be watchful and not distracted by the turmoil around him; and (3) do exactly what God told him to do.

When you begin to realize who Jesus Christ is and how much He cares for you, your faith level will increase. The greater your faith level, the clearer His strength will become.

Goals for the Day

- Read Joshua 1:1–9.
- Glance back at today's reading and review the three principles the angel of the Lord gave to Joshua.

Faith in Action

How can you implement these three principles in your own life?

_____

_____

_____

_____

_____

_____

_____

_____

Master, I choose to meditate on Your Word today instead of my own circumstances. I want to be watchful and not distracted by the turmoil around me. Help me to do exactly what You tell me to do. Increase my faith level today.

DAY 7

When You Stumble

SCRIPTURE READING: Matthew 14:22–33   KEY VERSE: Matthew 14:29

He said, "Come." And when Peter had come down out of the boat, he walked on the water to go to Jesus.

Many remember watching the news coverage of a young Olympic runner who fell as he came out of the backstretch before the final curve. Wrenching in pain, he tried to stand but collapsed back onto the track's surface.

A hush enveloped the crowd as eyes turned from the race's victor to the lone runner struggling to his feet at the far end of the stadium. Suddenly he was joined by an older man who eluded Olympic guards and jumped onto the track. It was the runner's father. Together, arm in arm, they pressed toward the finish line.

When Peter stepped out of the boat and began to walk on the water to Jesus, his one goal was to reach the Savior. And though the darkened waters caused his heart to momentarily doubt, Peter would not settle for defeat, and he called out, "Lord, save me!"

This is not an account of faithless peril. Had Peter truly doubted Jesus' power, he never would have gotten out of the boat. Never allow the enemy to tell you that you are worthless and defeated because you stumbled in your race to the finish line. Just like the loving father who ran to his son's side, Jesus runs to be near you and to carry you to victory.

Goals for the Day

- Read Matthew 14:22–33.
- Do you know someone who is struggling? Reach out to that person today and offer a word of encouragement.

Faith in Action

Do you get the sense that God is asking you to "get out of the boat" in some area of your life? What would it look like to take the first step?

_____

_____

_____

_____

_____

_____

_____

_____

_____

Precious Lord, thank You that when I stumble and fall, You are like the loving father who ran to his son's side. You are prepared to carry me on to victory. Together, we can make it to the finish line!

DAY 8

Fear or Faith?

SCRIPTURE READING: Matthew 8:23–27   KEY VERSE: 2 Timothy 1:7

God has not given us a spirit of fear, but of
power and of love and of a sound mind.

Wolf eels, which grow to be approximately six feet long, live in the cold waters of the northern Pacific Ocean in rocky dens on the seafloor. They have large, almost human-size eyes and formidable teeth, which give them a fierce appearance.

It is no wonder that for years, many marine scientists and divers believed them to be predatory and vicious. A recent discovery, however, has debunked that myth forever. Wolf eels actually use their long, sharp teeth to crack the shells of mollusks in order to get the meat inside. They do not bother humans at all. In fact, they are so docile that some have even played with the divers who studied them.

Something that looked fearful turned out not to be worthy of fear at all. Appearances can be deceiving, especially in spiritual matters. Peter was fine until he put his eyes on the waves at his feet and allowed the seeming impossibility of walking on water to rule his belief.

Jesus does not want you to evaluate situations with your senses and human reason, which can be led astray easily. He wants you to walk by spiritual sight that is guided by faith in the Lord who cannot fail.

Goals for the Day

- Read Matthew 8:23–27.
- Review the key verse of the day, 2 Timothy 1:7 . Circle any words that stand out to you. Spend time applying the truths of this passage to your specific fears.

Faith in Action

Write down your greatest fears in the space below. Considering today's reading, what is the wisest way to deal with those fears?

_____

_____

_____

_____

_____

_____

_____

_____

Dear heavenly Father, do not let me evaluate situations by my carnal senses and human reasoning. Let me walk by spiritual sight guided by faith in You—a God who can never fail!

DAY 9

The Faithfulness of God

SCRIPTURE READING: Psalm 102   KEY VERSES: Hebrews 13:5–6

Let your conduct be without covetousness; be content with such things as you have. For He Himself has said, "I will never leave you nor forsake you." So we may boldly say: "The Lord is my helper; I will not fear. What can man do to me?"

At times in our spiritual walk, we feel as though all of heaven is shut up before us. We find ourselves wondering whether God has forgotten us or we have done something to disappoint Him. But nothing we do surprises God. He is omniscient and perfectly in tune with our every thought.

God has chosen to love you, even in sin, with an unconditional love. His love is based not on your performance but on His grace. You could never in your own strength perform up to God's standards. He loves you just as much when you stumble and fall as He does when you closely follow Him. This is not an excuse for sin but an opportunity to learn to love Him better.

Along the pathway of faith each of us can expect to face times of trials and difficulty when it appears that God is distant and removed from us. Yet we walk not by sight but in the reality of the promise that He will never leave or forsake us (Heb. 13:5–6).

The times you feel God is doing nothing in your life are usually the very times He is doing His greatest work. Be of good courage; He may simply have you protected under the cover of His hand while He works out the necessary details for your advancement.

Goals for the Day

- Read Psalm 102.
- Identify places in today's Scripture reading when the psalmist showed honesty and transparency in his prayers. Let the psalmist's example guide your prayer time.

Faith in Action

What kind of prayer life do you aspire to have? Write down specifics. What steps can you take to have the prayer life you want?

_____

_____

_____

_____

_____

Almighty God, even when I feel You have forgotten me, You are still there. Thank You for Your unconditional love. I know You love me just as much when I stumble and fall as when I follow closely. Thank You for the great work You are doing in my life.

DAY 10

The Mind-Set of Faith

SCRIPTURE READING: Exodus 3:1–14   KEY VERSE: Exodus 3:14

God said to Moses, "I AM WHO I AM." And He said, "Thus you shall say to the children of Israel, 'I AM has sent me to you.'"

We often think faith begins when we step out and trust God for something He has promised, but actually faith begins even before this point. Faith is an attitude, a mind-set that has the power to chart our course through life.

Those who bypass faith in God experience discouragement because they are left to trust in their own abilities. What is human capability in light of God's omniscience?

Moses faced several critical points in his walk of faith. One came very early in his relationship with the Lord. The first time God spoke to Moses, He challenged Moses' ability to trust Him: "Come now, and I will send you to Pharaoh, so that you may bring My people, the sons of Israel, out of Egypt" (Ex. 3:10 NASB).

The situation appeared overwhelming to Moses. How could he possibly go to Pharaoh and tell him to let God's people go? He couldn't! At least, he couldn't in his own strength.

Moses felt totally inadequate to do what God wanted him to do. God understood. This is what is so endearing about our Savior; He understands our frailties. All He asks is for you to be willing. Trust His love and care, and be strengthened by His power.

Goals for the Day

- Read Exodus 3:1–14.
- Take some time to think more about this statement from today's reading, "Faith is an attitude, a mind-set that has the power to chart our course through life."

Faith in Action

Make a list of the tasks and responsibilities set before you. Write a prayer in the space below, asking God to give you His strength to fulfill your tasks and responsibilities.

Precious heavenly Father, thank You for understanding my frailties. Even when my pathway seems dark and unsure, I know You will strengthen me. I rest in Your love and care.

Faith is an attitude,

a mind-set that has

the power to chart our

course through life.

DAY 11

Growing Your Faith

SCRIPTURE READING: Matthew 17:14–20   KEY VERSE: Matthew 17:20

[Jesus said to them,] "Assuredly, I say to you, if you have faith as a mustard seed, you will say to this mountain, 'Move from here to there,' and it will move; and nothing will be impossible for you."

How do you respond when presented with a challenge that calls for a surge of faith in God? Hesitantly? Tentatively? Fearfully? Optimistically? The key to breaking the faith barrier and anchoring our trust in God is an exalted view of God Himself.

"But I thought to have more faith, I had to work at it more," you may say. You do, but your work is to see God for who He really is, not to struggle to obtain more faith or have a more positive mind-set.

When the disciples thirsted to have more faith, Jesus told them all that was necessary was faith the size of a mustard seed. "Use what you have," Jesus was saying, "and your faith will grow in the process."

We use what faith we have, as little as it may seem, by magnifying the heart's view of God. When Moses was scared to go to Pharaoh, God exploded Moses' worries with the revelation of Himself: "Thus you shall say to the sons of Israel, 'I AM has sent me to you'" (Ex. 3:14 NASB).

We grow in faith by seeing God in a new light. Our faith is as big as our God. If your notion of God is grand, your faith will soar.

Goals for the Day

- Read Matthew 17:14–20.
- Spend a few moments in prayer asking God to enlarge your vision of who He is.

Faith in Action

Write down what you believe to be true about God. Include His attributes and characteristics.

_____

_____

_____

_____

_____

_____

_____

Dear God, let my faith soar. Grow faith in me that is as big as You are. O God, I want to see You as You are. Shatter the obstacles of fear, disobedience, and faithlessness in my life. I want to break through the faith barrier.

DAY 12

Breaking the Faith Barrier

SCRIPTURE READING: Exodus 4   KEY VERSE: Hebrews 12:27

Now this, "Yet once more," indicates the removal of those things that are being shaken, as of things that are made, that the things which cannot be shaken may remain.

The journey of faith is not always safe; growing up in the Lord involves seasons of pain, testing, and uncertainty. Sometimes questions go unanswered for a long time. Penelope Stokes described the process in her book *Faith: The Substance of Things Unseen:*

> When we respond to the call to leave the walled garden and venture out into the woods beyond, we take the gamble of having our preconceived notions shattered. We open ourselves to new truth and new ways of perceiving; we embrace "the removing of what can be shaken . . . so that what cannot be shaken may remain" (Hebrews 12:27). We commit ourselves to exploration . . .
>
> If we intend to be spiritual explorers, to follow the unknown paths and journey into unmarked territory, we must learn to trust God. Like Christian in *The Pilgrim's Progress,* we must put our hands to our ears, shut out the voices that would call us back to safety and sameness, and run with all our might toward the woods, where God waits to lead us on our way.

We need to embrace our own explorations, even when we can't please everybody, even when others are afraid we are taking the wrong path . . . even if we risk falling down the mountain and breaking an arm in the process.[1]

Goals for the Day

- Read Exodus 4.
- Spend some time today thinking about Moses' choice between entertaining his doubts and fears and moving forward in obedience to God.

Faith in Action

In today's Bible reading, Moses was so fearful he said, "Please, Lord, send someone else." And yet, Moses ultimately obeyed. Why do you think Moses was able to move forward in faith?

_____

_____

_____

_____

O Lord, help me shut out the voices that call me back to safety and sameness. I want to run with all my might to where You wait to lead me on my way. Let me move forward by faith to explore and penetrate unmarked territory.

DAY 13

MATTERS OF FAITH

SCRIPTURE READING: Exodus 5   KEY VERSE: Isaiah 55:9

*For as the heavens are higher than the earth,
so are My ways higher than your ways, and
My thoughts than your thoughts.*

You did something kind for a neighbor, and your gesture was considered to be self-serving. You put in extra hours on a project at work helping a coworker in a bind, and others said you were just trying to look good to your boss. It hurts when people misunderstand your intentions. Not only is the good effect lost in the process, but you end up with blame you don't deserve.

Think about how Moses felt. He was God's special messenger on a divinely appointed mission of mercy, and the people accused him of trying to make their lives more miserable. They were absolutely wrong, as they would later discover, but in the meantime submissive Moses caught the brunt of their grumbling.

Such misinterpretations often happen in matters of faith. Why? God's ways do not always make sense in a sinful world. His methods sometimes turn human reasoning on its head or go against popular opinion. And sometimes the benefits or rewards of obedience are delayed or delivered in a way that nonbelievers cannot recognize.

If others mock you for doing what the Lord says instead of walking in the world's path, you can stand firm. The true and ultimate victory belongs to Him.

Goals for the Day

- Read Exodus 5.
- Review the key verse of the day, Isaiah 55:9. Spend some time today thinking about this passage and how it relates to the situations in life that you might not understand.

Faith in Action

Make a list of the situations that cause you to question or doubt. Spend time in prayer asking God to give you clarity.

_____

_____

_____

_____

_____

_____

Dear heavenly Father, even though Your ways don't always make sense to my human reasoning, I know the ultimate victory belongs to You. Let me stand firm in this knowledge and walk Your way instead of the pathways of this sinful world.

DAY 14

SUFFERING A FAITH FAILURE

SCRIPTURE READING: Numbers 13–14   KEY VERSES: Proverbs 3:5–6

Trust in the LORD with all your heart, and lean not on your own understanding; in all your ways acknowledge Him, and He shall direct your paths.

The spies' report was very negative and discouraging. The Israelites spent the entire night weeping and mourning. The situation seemed hopeless.

Under God's direction, Moses had led them triumphantly out of Egypt toward their final destination—the promised land. But now they were stuck in the desert outside a land filled with menacing giants.

At a critical point in time—the moment of challenge—the Israelites took their eyes off the Lord and looked only at the obstacles. Because they forgot God's promise and listened to false information, an entire generation wandered and died in the desert, never even getting a glimpse of the land of milk and honey.

Are you facing a challenge to your faith? Is God calling you to a task that seems unreasonable? Don't assess the situation by your limited resources; failure to see things God's way may cause you to miss His blessing, and others may be hurt. Disobedience is always followed by disappointment and disillusionment.

Remember what God has done for you in the past, and trust Him to deal with the impossible. You cannot be defeated when you follow God's plan in confident faith.

Goals for the Day

- Read Numbers 13–14.
- At a critical point, the Israelites took their eyes off God and focused on their obstacles. Identify the situations where you are prone to do the same.

Faith in Action

Write down a few of the high points in your history with God. How has God come through for you in unexpected ways?

_____

_____

_____

_____

_____

_____

Precious Father, as I face my spiritual journey today, help me view each challenge in terms of Your resources instead of my limited strength. Give me faith to deal with the impossible.

DAY 15

Facing Giants

SCRIPTURE READING: 1 Samuel 17:1–11   KEY VERSE: 1 John 5:4

Whatever is born of God overcomes the world. And this is the victory that has overcome the world—our faith.

Tomorrow she has to face the committee and tell them what she thinks. Last month they asked her to review books for a children's reading club, and she feels that three of the books are detrimental and advocate unbiblical values. She also knows that most of the committee members are not believers and will not understand her arguments.

As she thinks about the conflict to come, panic sets in. It isn't until she recalls past victories in the Lord that she calms down and recognizes that the battle is really His.

Look at David's words of positive confession before he faced the sneering giant Goliath: "The LORD who delivered me from the paw of the lion and from the paw of the bear, He will deliver me from the hand of this Philistine" (1 Sam. 17:37 NASB).

David could say with unwavering confidence that God would give him the resounding victory. He called to mind former defenseless times when God delivered him from destruction, and he relied on God's might to do it again.

What giant looms in your future? What battle are you headed for today? Are you claiming the victory right now in His name? Always remember—you know the God who conquers.

Goals for the Day

- Read 1 Samuel 17:1–11.
- Spend a few moments identifying the "giants" in your life. Glance back at 1 Samuel 17:37 and read David's positive confession.

Faith in Action

In the space below, follow David's example and write down a "positive confession" that speaks to the challenges in your life.

___

Father God, there are giants ahead—tremendous battles to face. Give me the faith that conquers. I claim the victory right now in Your name.

DAY 16

Victory Through Faith

Scripture Reading: 1 Samuel 17:12–37   KEY Verse: Philippians 1:6

Being confident of this very thing, that He who has begun a good work in you will complete it until the day of Jesus Christ.

As a young shepherd boy, David did not possess all the qualities of a strong, conquering faith. God took years to train him for his future role as a king of Israel. However, he never lost sight of God's goal for his life by fretting over the future.

When facing his first major challenge with Goliath, David mentally went through several steps to ensure himself of the victory through faith:

Recall past victories. David remembered God's past faithfulness and was encouraged.

Reaffirm the reasons for the conflict. Make sure your motives and heart are pure before God.

Reject discouragement. Always be wary of pessimism. Instead, practice recalling God's promises to you.

Recognize the true nature of the battle. Claim your position in Christ as a joint heir and a beloved child of God.

Respond with positive confessions of faith. God is in control, and He will give you the victory.

Rely on God. All your hope and security is in Christ. You struggle with human abilities and limitations, but God knows no limits.

Reckon the victory. David did, and you can too! Whether the victory comes today or in ten years, God will complete what He has begun in your life (Phil. 1:6).

Goals for the Day

- Read 1 Samuel 17:12–37.
- Look over today's reading and review the steps that David took before confronting Goliath. Pick out a couple of these steps to implement in your own life.

Faith in Action

Write down a specific Scripture passage that will help you confront discouragement.

_____

_____

_____

_____

_____

Dear Lord, thank You for past victories. As I face the battles of life, make my motives pure. Help me resist discouragement and claim my position as a joint heir with Christ. Your power knows no limit, and You will complete what You have started in my life.

DAY 17

CONQUERING FAITH

SCRIPTURE READING: 1 Samuel 17:38–51   KEY VERSE: 1 Samuel 17:45

David said to the Philistine, "You come to me with a sword, with a spear, and with a javelin. But I come to you in the name of the LORD of hosts, the God of the armies of Israel, whom you have defied."

David's faith may seem to be of an almost superhuman kind—one beyond reach—if you focus on the feats he accomplished. Killing a giant with only some stones and a slingshot seems unbelievable.

But that is exactly the point. It was impossible and unbelievable. David's simple, childlike faith in almighty God produced the decisive victory for the Israelites that brought much glory to their Lord's name.

The faith David had—conquering faith—is yours when you understand the true nature of his trust in God. Conquering faith is a faith that rejects the discouraging words of others.

What if David had listened to the taunts and questions of his brothers, or what if he had let Saul's doubts coerce him to wear cumbersome, oversize armor? David knew that if he obeyed God and let Him work, success was the only possible outcome.

Conquering faith also recognizes the true nature of the battle. When Goliath in arrogance came against the army of God, the issue became spiritual, and David understood this principle immediately.

Are you facing a spiritual "Goliath" right now? God does not expect you to manage the situation on your own. Ask Him to handle the conflict. Conquering faith knows the One for the job.

Goals for the Day

- Read 1 Samuel 17:38–51.
- Spend some time thinking about the role faith plays in pursuing your passions, goals, and God-given purpose.

Faith in Action

Why is "conquering faith" necessary to fulfill God's purposes for your life?

_____

_____

_____

_____

_____

_____

_____

Heavenly Father, give me conquering faith—a faith that rejects discouraging words from others and recognizes the true nature of the battle. Handle my conflicts. Defeat my spiritual Goliaths.

DAY 18

FAITH WHEN GOD SAYS NO

SCRIPTURE READING: 2 Samuel 12:1–23 KEY VERSES: Psalm 138:7–8

Though I walk in the midst of trouble, You will revive me; You will stretch out Your hand against the wrath of my enemies, and Your right hand will save me. The LORD will perfect that which concerns me; Your mercy, O LORD, endures forever; do not forsake the works of Your hands.

The prophet Nathan came to David and, under the direction of God's Spirit, spoke words that convicted David's heart of the guilt he bore and the sin he had committed against the Lord. The days that followed the event were filled with tension and despair as David learned that Bathsheba was carrying his child—a child that God had already revealed would die.

The heartache, the misery—none of us can truly know how deeply this man suffered. Not only had he hurt family and friends, but he had grieved Someone much nearer and dearer than his earthly companions—the Lord Himself.

But in the midst of this tragedy, don't miss the sensitivity of David's relationship with God. When the king received news that the child would surely die, he went straight to the Lord in prayer. That was the one place David knew he could find forgiveness and restoration.

When a person is broken in sin, he is not alone. God is with him, and He is quick to restore the person's fellowship with Him when he acknowledges his sin. You can praise God for His sovereignty in your life, even in times when His answer to your prayer is no. He will always give you His best at just the right time.

Goals for the Day

- Read 2 Samuel 12:1–23.
- Look up 1 John 1:9 in your Bible and use it to guide your prayer time.

Faith in Action

Unconfessed sin will steal your peace. If you have fallen into habitual unconfessed sin, write a prayer below asking God to forgive and restore you.

___

Father, I rejoice that You are sovereign over every detail of my life. Even when Your answer to my prayer is no, I know You will give me Your best at the right time.

DAY 19

FAITH TO DREAM

SCRIPTURE READING: Psalm 71:13–21   KEY VERSE: 2 Corinthians 5:7

We walk by faith, not by sight.

When God gives you a promise for the future, He is responsible for opening the right door at the right time for you to accomplish the task. Author and teacher Henrietta Mears taught her students to dream. In life, she did just that and turned an unheard-of Sunday school department at First Presbyterian in Hollywood, California, into a program that drew thousands into a deeper walk of faith in Christ.

However, in 1937 she faced an interesting problem. Her ever-increasing youth program had outgrown its retreat facilities. God made it clear—He would provide a new retreat area that would meet the need.

Property, once an elaborate resort, in the San Bernardino Mountains became available. But the price, even though greatly reduced, was still too high. Yet, Henrietta knew if this was God's meeting place, He would provide the means to purchase it.[2]

The owner's poor health along with a damaging storm opened the way for the purchase of the property at an "unheard-of" low price. Henrietta concluded that the way of faith is never by sight or human reason; it is always by the sovereignty of God.

Is there a need in your life that seems overwhelming? Trust God; He has His best in store for you.

Goals for the Day

- Read Psalm 71:13–21.
- Today's reading teaches that we should dream big whenever God is involved. Give yourself permission to set apart time today to "dream big." What types of dreams ignite your passion and give you a sense of purpose?

Faith in Action

What comes to mind when you "dream big?" What awesome goal is God calling you to accomplish that is impossible apart from His grace and blessing?

_____

_____

_____

_____

_____

_____

_____

O God, give me the ability to dream big. Remove all that limits my vision. Let me see beyond natural circumstances that restrict my faith.

When God gives you a

promise for the future,

He is responsible for

opening the right door

at the right time for you

to accomplish the task.

DAY 20

Obeying in Faith

Scripture Reading: Luke 5:1–11   KEY Verse: Luke 5:5

Simon answered and said to Him, "Master, we have toiled all night and caught nothing; nevertheless at Your word I will let down the net."

Jesus was speaking to a group gathered along the shores of Galilee. When He finished, He turned to Peter and told him to raise the boat's sails, head back out into the open water, and lower his nets for a large catch of fish.

Tired and wishing only for a few hours of rest, Peter seemed to hesitate. Did Jesus know what He was requesting? Everyone there knew the best time for fishing—especially with nets—was at night; the worst time was during the day.

Peter tried to reason: "Master, we worked hard all night and caught nothing." But Jesus remained firm: "Let down your nets for a catch" (Luke 5:4–5 NASB).

Every time we are called to obey God, our faith is challenged and our true nature revealed. The miracle of the tremendous quantity of fish was the result of Peter's willingness to trust and obey Christ by faith. In obedience he replied, "I will do as you say and let down the nets" (Luke 5:5 NASB).

When our hearts are set on obedience, God responds mightily. There will be moments in life when you may ask, "Lord, is this a matter of obedience?" If so, choose to obey in faith, then "let down your nets" and prepare for a tremendous blessing.

Goals for the Day

- Read Luke 5:1–11.
- Spend time in prayer asking God to reveal any areas where you have failed to obey Him. Ask God for strength to submit to Him in every circumstance.

Faith in Action

Can you recall a time when you failed to obey God? What were the consequences? If you were confronted with that same situation again, what would you do differently?

_____

_____

_____

_____

_____

_____

Lord, I set my heart this day to obey Your Word. As I move forward in obedience, I am "letting down my nets" spiritually and preparing for a tremendous blessing. I know it is coming, so thank You in advance!

DAY 21

The Test of Faith

SCRIPTURE READING: James 1:2–8   KEY VERSE: James 1:12

Blessed is the man who endures temptation; for when he has been approved, he will receive the crown of life which the Lord has promised to those who love Him.

Most of us know the story of Joseph and the depth of his faith. Genesis 39–50 records the events of his life and how God provided emotional strength for him to rise above discouragement. The principle involved in Joseph's life is one of extreme faith.

He didn't enjoy being sold into bondage. Like any of us, he probably fought feelings of rejection, loneliness, and fear. He had worshiped and trusted God. Yet he ended up in a foreign land with no immediate hope of returning home to his family. Even there, Joseph held fast to his conviction—God had a plan for his life. He had been given a vision, and he refused to fall prey to sin and discontentment.

Each of us will face times of trial and discouragement. But it is here among life's darker moments that God exposes the depth of our faith.

For Joseph to testify to God's faithfulness, there had to be an Egyptian encounter. For you to affirm the eternal love and strength of God, there must be a test of faith in your life as well. Remember, God will never abandon you. Just as He was with Joseph, He is with you—forever!

Goals for the Day

- Read James 1:2–8.
- Spend time in prayer asking God to give you strength for the temptations and trials you are currently experiencing.

Faith in Action

Think about the biggest test of faith you've endured. Write down the lessons you learned from that trial. How can those lessons equip you for the challenges you are currently facing?

_____

_____

_____

_____

_____

_____

_____

Precious Lord, despite the feelings of rejection, loneliness, and fear that sometimes flood my soul, I know You have a plan for me. Through all my trials, expose and then strengthen the depth of my faith.

DAY 22

Trusting God

Scripture Reading: Genesis 39   KEY Verse: Genesis 39:23

The keeper of the prison did not look into anything that was under Joseph's authority, because the Lord was with him; and whatever he did, the Lord made it prosper.

People who have spent time in prison talk about the mind-numbing effects of incarceration. Days slide into days, months into months, and an inmate's perception of time and reality may become stunted. It is easy to lose motivation or the will to live without hope, a goal, something to work toward.

Such was not the case with Joseph. If ever anyone had a reason to be bitter, it was Joseph. He did not even deserve to be in jail. Joseph could have allowed his frustration to deepen into resentment and then taken it out on his fellow prisoners and the guards. He could have made life miserable. Instead, Joseph chose to trust God:

> But the Lord was with Joseph and extended kindness to him, and gave him favor in the sight of the chief jailer. And the chief jailer committed to Joseph's charge all the prisoners who were in the jail; so that whatever was done there, he was responsible for it. The chief jailer did not supervise anything under Joseph's charge because the Lord was with him; and whatever he did, the Lord made to prosper. (Gen. 39:21–23 nasb)

Joseph understood that God's plans for him extended beyond the negatives of the here and now; in faith he could look past the present pain, and as a result, God turned his circumstances into a beautiful testimony of His love and provision.

Goals for the Day

- Read Genesis 39.
- Spend time in prayer asking God to give you favor in your current circumstances.

Faith in Action

Joseph had good reason to feel bitter, but he wisely chose not to be. Do you feel resentment because of past hurts? Write down your feelings below and ask God to help you deal with bitterness.

_____

_____

_____

_____

_____

I trust You, Master! By faith, I look beyond the past and present into the tremendous future You have planned for me. Turn my negative circumstances into a testimony of Your love and provision.

DAY 23

Faithful Obedience

Scripture Reading: 1 Peter 1:1–15   Key Verse: 1 Peter 1:7

The genuineness of your faith, being much more precious than gold that perishes, though it is tested by fire, may be found to praise, honor, and glory at the revelation of Jesus Christ.

Though Joseph was sold into slavery, he refused to become embittered. As a result, God blessed him through Potiphar, an Egyptian officer who purchased him. He was taken into Potiphar's home and given great responsibility. The Bible tells us that Joseph was a successful man (Gen. 39:2). All that Potiphar had was left in Joseph's care.

However, what happened next in Joseph's life was certainly a test of his character and obedience to God. It is fairly common for God to test our level of obedience. One day as Joseph was going about his duties, Potiphar's wife approached him with an alluring temptation. She wanted Joseph to commit adultery with her, but Joseph immediately recognized the error and refused her advances.

Joseph said, "How then could I do this great evil, and sin against God?" (Gen. 39:9 NASB). His first thought was what such a sin would do to his relationship with God. Obedience was far more important to Joseph than a moment of physical pleasure.

Potiphar's wife was furious and turned on him by lying to her husband. Potiphar had Joseph imprisoned. However, God was with him, orchestrating the circumstances of his life for even greater blessing.

If you are facing a situation that involves temptation, ask yourself, Am I about to do something that will lead to my ruin or damage my faith? Then remember that faithful obedience always leads to blessing.

Goals for the Day

- Read 1 Peter 1:1–15.
- Write down 1 Peter 1:5–7 on a notecard and spend a few minutes each day committing it to memory.

Faith in Action

Think about these words from today's reading: "Faithful obedience always leads to blessing." Why do you think that is true?

_____

_____

_____

_____

_____

Precious Lord, thank You for the faith already instilled in my heart. Help me continue growing stronger each day in my spiritual journey of faith.

DAY 24

FAITH TO CLING TO

SCRIPTURE READING: Genesis 7   KEY VERSE: Hebrews 11:7

By faith Noah, being divinely warned of things not yet seen, moved with godly fear, prepared an ark for the saving of his household, by which he condemned the world and became heir of the righteousness which is according to faith.

It is an old saying that people are "creatures of habit." Of course, we love occasional variation in the routine, but we strive for stability as much as possible. If you ever feel stressed when dealing with the unknown, then you have a small idea of how Noah felt when God told him to build an ark. An ark? He probably didn't have a clear idea of what it even looked like until God's blueprint began to take shape.

In a single encounter, Noah's concept of daily life took a violent twist. Though he was surrounded by a self-serving, sensual society with no interest in God, he knew where he and his family stood. But suddenly his vision of the future changed forever. No more neighbors, no towns, no noise of crowds, no marketplace—what would the world be like?

Hebrews 11:7 (NASB) notes that in spite of the questions: "By faith Noah, being warned by God about things not yet seen, in reverence prepared an ark for the salvation of his household . . . and became an heir of the righteousness which is according to faith."

Faith was all he could cling to; God was literally his only port in the storm. When your circumstances turn upside down, when you don't have the answers, trust the Lord. His plan is perfect.

Goals for the Day

- Read Genesis 7.
- Spend a few moments contemplating Noah's obedience. What motivated Noah to obey? What would've happened if he didn't?

Faith in Action

Living a life of purpose and peace is contingent on obeying God—even when it doesn't make sense. Is there a situation in your life where God is calling you to obey?

_____

_____

_____

_____

_____

_____

Almighty God, You are my port in every storm of life. When my circumstances are confusing, when I don't have all the answers, help me trust You. Your plan is always perfect.

DAY 25

The Foundation of Faith

Scripture Reading: Matthew 7:24–29   Key Verse: Romans 8:35

Who shall separate us from the love of Christ? Shall tribulation, or distress, or persecution, or famine, or nakedness, or peril, or sword?

Imagine that someone walked up to you today and said, "Here's ten million dollars. Build yourself a dream house." Chances are, you're not going to pick a poor lot filled with sand. You're not going to use the cheapest, knottiest, half-rotted lumber you can find. Of course not. You search for the choicest acreage and the highest-quality building materials you can afford.

But when it comes to constructing a sturdy foundation for their lives, many people settle for inferior supplies—possessions, fame, or financial security. On the surface, these things seem reliable enough, but in the hard blast of a personal crisis they crumble away. A fire can eat up possessions; fame can disappear with one piece of negative press; a failing economy or a layoff can destroy financial security.

That's why Jesus wanted you to see beyond the temporal to the eternal. He said, "Everyone who hears these words of Mine and acts upon them may be compared to a wise man who built his house upon the rock . . . The winds blew, and slammed against that house; and yet it did not fall" (Matt. 7:24–25 nasb).

You need the shake-proof foundation of Christ to make it through the storms of life (Rom. 8:35). Only on His sure footing can you find security that survives every trouble. Build your life on the foundation of faith—Jesus Christ.

Goals for the Day

- Read Matthew 7:24–29.
- Spend a few moments in prayer giving thanks to God for being a trustworthy and solid foundation.

Faith in Action

What type of foundation have you built your life on? Are there changes you need to make?

_____

_____

_____

_____

_____

_____

Dear God, I do not want to build with inferior supplies—possessions, fame, or financial security—because these things crumble. Empower me to build my life upon the foundations of Your Word and Your Son, Jesus Christ.

DAY 26

THE HUMBLE STEP OF FAITH

SCRIPTURE READING: 2 Kings 5   KEY VERSES: 1 Peter 5:5–6

You younger people, submit yourselves to your elders. Yes, all of you be submissive to one another, and be clothed with humility, for "God resists the proud, but gives grace to the humble." Therefore humble yourselves under the mighty hand of God, that He may exalt you in due time.

Sometimes great examples of faith come in small, unappealing packages. For Naaman, the leprous captain of the army of Syria, his moment of faith came when he dipped in dirty water far from home. Naaman was insulted. After all the trouble it took to travel to a foreign country, the prophet he came to see did not greet him as a proper host should. Even worse, Elisha sent him orders by a lowly servant to wash in the Jordan.

Naaman was so outraged by Elisha's supposed affront that he refused to perform the one act that would save him from his ravaging disease. Finally, his servants came to talk him out of his pride. They asked him pointedly: "Had the prophet told you to do some great thing, would you not have done it? How much more then, when he says to you, 'Wash and be clean'?" (2 Kings 5:13 NASB).

When Naaman paused to consider their words, he realized that his refusal to humble himself before God would cost his life. He hurried to obey Elisha's instructions from the Lord, and his flesh was made whole.

Do you say yes to God in the little things? Are you content to follow His will when you do not receive any of the glory? No matter what the task, God always rewards the humble step of faith.

Goals for the Day

- Read 2 Kings 5.
- Spend a few minutes thinking about how Naaman almost lost his life because of pride. How is pride a threat in your spiritual life?

Faith in Action

How would you describe the difference between humility and pride? What are the outcomes of each?

_____

_____

_____

_____

Father God, make me content to follow Your will, even when I do not receive any glory. No matter how small or great the task, let me step forth in humble faith.

DAY 27

Unshakable Faith

Scripture Reading: John 20:24–39   KEY Verse: John 20:29

Jesus said to him, "Thomas, because you have seen Me, you have believed. Blessed are those who have not seen and yet have believed."

The apostle Thomas felt deserted. The One he had followed closely and served for almost three years was gone. A cold cave of stone held Jesus' battered, torn body, and no one knew what to do next.

Later that Sabbath when Thomas arrived at the disciples' meeting, their mood had changed completely. "We have seen the Lord!" they cried. But Thomas couldn't share their enthusiasm. He had not seen the Lord, and he did not want to be set up for yet another disappointment. His focus was gone, his grand vision of the future shattered, and his faith shaken.

Have you been there? A negative experience left a bad impression, and you are afraid to trust again. One more letdown, and you aren't sure how you might respond. If you could have a glimpse of God in the dark times, you would have hope.

Jesus met Thomas right where he was in wavering faith. The living Christ stood before him face-to-face and told him to feel His hands and side. Thomas responded with one of the most moving confessions of faith in Scripture: "My Lord and my God!" (John 20:28 NASB).

Look at Jesus. He is real, and He is there to meet you in the bleakest hour. You will have the same reply when you see Him as He is.

Goals for the Day

- Read John 20:24–39.
- Spend a few moments considering Thomas's story. Identify the areas in your life where you are prone to doubt.

Faith in Action

Jesus invited Thomas to come closer and examine His scarred hands. In what areas do you think Jesus might be inviting you to draw closer?

_____

_____

_____

_____

_____

_____

_____

_____

O Lord, sometimes the shadows of the past make me afraid to trust. During these dark times, meet me where I am. Let me see You as You are. Let me touch You with the hand of faith.

DAY 28

The Way of Faith

Scripture Reading: Hebrews 11   KEY Verse: Hebrews 11:6

Without faith it is impossible to please Him, for he who comes to God must believe that He is, and that He is a rewarder of those who diligently seek Him.

Hebrews 11 is an emotional chapter. Spread before you are the spiritual sagas of generations who placed their unwavering trust in God, who took them on adventures beyond their imaginations. Some never saw the end result of their faith, but a great many did. Do you notice some common denominators among their experiences? No matter how different their particular stories might have been, certain principles held true for them all.

Faith was the way of trials. Noah certainly didn't ask for the ridicule and doubt of his neighbors. Moses would have preferred an easier way out of Egypt. But God used the rough times to sharpen them for the future and to be an even more powerful testimony to others.

Faith was the way of the most misunderstanding. Abraham's choice to follow God wherever He led was surely confusing to some. It didn't make sense from an earthly point of view for Rahab to hide the Israelite spies. From God's perspective, however, their unquestioning obedience opened the door to His blessing.

Faith was the way of patience. David had to wait many years

before God fulfilled His promise of giving him the kingship. And many of the believers of the New Testament were put to death after prolonged periods of persecution. God's ultimate rewards for them were (and are) worth the wait.

Goals for the Day

- Read Hebrews 11.
- Review the verse of the day, Hebrews 11:6. Circle any words or phrases that stand out to you in this passage.

Faith in Action

Which of the stories in Hebrews 11 most inspire you? Why?

_____

_____

_____

_____

_____

_____

_____

Dear heavenly Father, I realize that the way of faith is often a journey of trials. Use the rough times to prepare me for the future. Give me patience to endure the darkest hours.

DAY 29

STANDING IN FAITH

SCRIPTURE READING: Daniel 6   KEY VERSE: Hebrews 11:33

Who through faith subdued kingdoms, worked righteousness, obtained promises, stopped the mouths of lions.

A plot was afoot. Some political advisers decided it was time to put a negative spin on the efforts of one of the chief officials, to make sure he was put in the bad graces of the executive in chief. Their plan worked. The official's loyalties were cast into question, and it wasn't long before he paid the price.

That sounds as if it could be part of a plot for a modern novel, but it's really a very old story about how Daniel came to be in the lions' den. Daniel took a stand of obedience by refusing to pray to anyone besides the Lord God, and his decision ran in the face of the new law that demanded worship of King Darius alone for thirty days.

Taking a stand in faith very often entails negative consequences, at least from an earthly perspective. Those who do not honor God as Lord are usually angered by those who do, and radical displays of humble reliance on Him can incense them even more.

If you have ever been the victim of harassment by peers, "friends," coworkers, or supervisors as a result of sticking by a scriptural conviction, then you understand a little of what Daniel felt. You have probably not experienced retribution this dire in your own life, but the principle is the same. God will turn negative response into something for His glory. God shut the mouths of the lions, and He can silence your detractors as well.

Goals for the Day

- Read Daniel 6.
- Spend a few moments thinking about Daniel's story. In what ways can you relate to him?

Faith in Action

Today's reading said, "God shut the mouths of lions, and He can silence your detractors as well." Write a prayer below asking God to deal with the "lions" in your life.

_____

_____

_____

_____

_____

_____

I take my stand, Lord! I honor You as Lord of my life. I rely on You to turn the negative to positive in every area of my life. You plead my cause. I rest my case with You.

God will turn negative response into something for His glory. God shut the mouths of the lions, and He can silence your detractors as well.

DAY 30

Barriers to a Purposeful Life

Scripture Reading: Psalm 25   Key Verse: Psalm 25:14

*The secret of the Lord is with those who fear Him,
and He will show them His covenant.*

Barriers to faith keep us from accomplishing God's will. A poor self-image; ignorance of who God is; doubt; feelings of inadequacy; fear of failure; selfish desires and actions—all contribute to a lack of faith in God. This is because anytime our eyes of faith drift from Jesus Christ to ourselves or our circumstances, we lose our spiritual focus. At some point, everyone fights feelings of doubt and low self-esteem. However, these are feelings, and they have nothing to do with truth.

Jesus was quick to point out that Satan is the father of lies (John 8:44). He is relentless in his attempt to draw you away from God. Whispering thoughts of doubt and feelings of self-pity easily assist his disabling work.

How can you break through barriers to faith such as the ones just mentioned?

First, learn to listen only to God. If you are unsure of what you are hearing, go to God's Word and ask Him to reveal His will to you.

Second, be courageous and not afraid to trust God. He has never failed anyone, and He won't fail you.

Third, when He tells you to go forward in faith, do it, and allow Him to take care of the consequences of your obedience.

Fourth, once you have obeyed God, look for evidence of His blessing in your life. Obedience is the gateway to blessing, and God blesses those who honor Him with their lives.

Goals for the Day

- Read Psalm 25.
- Spend a few moments in prayer asking God to reveal obstacles that are keeping you from moving forward in His purpose for your life.

Faith in Action

What lies are you prone to believe that prevent you from moving forward in faith? How can the four steps from today's reading help you overcome them?

_____

_____

_____

Father, I choose to listen for Your voice and trust You in every circumstance. Let this day be one of new direction in my spiritual journey as I move forward in faith and obedience.

DAY 31

JOURNEY OUT OF EGYPT

SCRIPTURE READING: Exodus 19   KEY VERSE: Exodus 19:4

You have seen what I did to the Egyptians, and how I bore you on eagles' wings and brought you to Myself.

For 430 years God's people were enslaved in Egypt until Moses came with God's powerful declaration of deliverance: "Let my people go!" (Ex. 5:1). Israel's dramatic journey out of Egypt is symbolic of our deliverance from sin, and God's message to us today is the same as to Israel. He wants a separated people: "Come out from among them and be separate, says the Lord. Do not touch what is unclean, and I will receive you" (2 Cor. 6:17).

Part of living a life of purpose, passion, and peace means being delivered from the power of sin. It is time to leave the bondage of spiritual Egypt behind. It doesn't matter how many times in the past you tried and failed. This time it will be different. The light of God's Word points the way, and He will bear you up on eagles' wings.

Goals for the Day

- Read Exodus 19.
- Take a few moments to identify the sins you are struggling most with during this season of life.

Faith in Action

Today's reading said, "Part of living a life of purpose, passion, and peace means being delivered from the power of sin." Write a prayer below asking God to help you overcome any sins that are holding you back and keeping you in bondage.

_____

_____

_____

_____

_____

_____

_____

_____

_____

_____

Father, I confess that I have habitual sins in my life. I ask in Jesus' name that You will deliver me from anything that is holding me back from doing Your will and living the life You want me to live.

DAY 32

Walking by Faith

Scripture Reading: Romans 8:35–39   Key Verse: Romans 8:37

*In all these things we are more than conquerors
through Him who loved us.*

Do you ever worry about whether you can trust God? Many deny it, but their actions speak differently. Have you ever prayed for something and felt as though your prayers were going unanswered? After a while, it is easy to think that maybe it would be okay to help God out—give Him a little shove to start things off. But you may want to consider the following:

God is sovereign. He is both personal and loving. He has not forgotten you. Even though you may have to wait for the answer to your prayers, when it comes, it will be a wondrous blessing because you were willing to wait and trust the Lord for the answer.

God is infinitely wise. All knowledge about all things belongs to Him. He knows everything. Deep love and commitment toward those who have accepted His Son as their Savior are hallmarks of His personal care. Therefore, He has provided a way for sin to be eradicated from your life. In wisdom and mercy, He desires for you to live free of the bondage of sin and failure.

God loves perfectly and completely. He can meet all your needs. You may wonder how this can be, especially since you can't see or touch Him. Deep within the resources of His love, contentment and a sense of peace are waiting just for you. Nothing the world offers can duplicate these things.

Goals for the Day

- Read Romans 8:35–39.
- Review the key verse of the day, Romans 8:37. Write it on a notecard or on your phone. Next to the Scripture, right down a paraphrase of the verse in your own words.

Faith in Action

Think about the points from today's reading: God is sovereign, God is infinitely wise, and God loves perfectly and completely. Which of these truths resonate most deeply right now?

_____

_____

_____

_____

_____

Father God, You are sovereign and wise. You know everything about my life. You love me perfectly and completely and have the ability to meet all my needs. Thank You that You have not forgotten me!

DAY 33

The Truth About Sin

Scripture Reading: Romans 7:18–25   Key Verse: Romans 5:12

*Just as through one man sin entered the
world, and death through sin, and thus death
spread to all men, because all sinned.*

Man's natural state is one of sinfulness. It is a direct result of the fall, and the rebellion Adam and Eve demonstrated in the garden of Eden. Our fallen nature is evident in feelings and emotions such as jealousy, anger, fear, resentment, lack of forgiveness, lust, and more. If sin isn't dealt with, it will negatively impact our relationship with God and prevent us from living the life God intends.

When the apostle Paul became aware of the depth of his sin, he cried out, "Wretched man that I am! Who will set me free from the body of this death?" [meaning spiritual death] (Rom. 7:24 nasb).

Coming face-to-face with our sinfulness should bring the same response from us. If we were left on our own with no thought of God, sin would control our lives. Only by the grace of God and the mercy of Jesus Christ can we say with the apostle Paul, "Thanks be to God through Jesus Christ our Lord!" (Rom. 7:25 nasb).

Only Jesus Christ can save us from the clutches of sin. Only He can change the nature of our hearts and give us a new life. We can choose to live for Him and turn from evil, but first we must come to a point where we see our sin as He sees it. Nothing is glamorous about sin. It keeps us from experiencing all that God has for us.

Goals for the Day

- Read Romans 7:18–25.
- Ask God to surface anything in your life that reflects the old sinful nature. Pray to walk faithfully in the grace He provides in Jesus.

Faith in Action

Write down any thoughts that came to mind during your prayer time. Are there any unconfessed sins you need to deal with?

_____

_____

_____

_____

_____

_____

Dear Lord, thank You for saving me from the clutches of sin, changing my nature, and giving me new life. I choose to live for You and turn from evil. Surface anything in my life that reflects the old, sinful nature. Then help me walk faithfully in the grace provided through Jesus.

DAY 34

How to Deal with Sin

Scripture Reading: Romans 6:15–23   Key Verse: Romans 6:22

Now having been set free from sin, and having become slaves of God, you have your fruit to holiness, and the end, everlasting life.

You accepted Jesus Christ as your Lord and Savior, recognizing that He paid the penalty for your sins on the cross. You know that you're forgiven, cleansed, and righteous in God's eyes. But still, a particular sin plagues you. You think it's gone and the fight is over, but the temptation comes back. You cave in again at a moment of weakness or a time when your guard is down. Maybe you even wonder how God can still love you.

You're not alone. Paul expressed the same sentiment of frustration and exasperation. He said, "For the good that I want, I do not do, but I practice the very evil that I do not want" (Rom. 7:19 NASB). Paul knew that even though he was saved, the power of sin was still there, doing daily battle with his new nature.

What is the solution? First, you must see your sin, including recurring sin, for what it is—an offense against a holy God that can be removed only by the blood of Jesus. Confess the specific sin to Him, and refuse to become entangled by false guilt. You're forgiven freely.

Remember that you belong to Him completely; nothing else has the power to hold you captive. Turn to the One who frees you from sin when temptation strikes, and you will win every time.

Goals for the Day

- Read Romans 6:15–23.
- Spend a few minutes thinking about how you have dealt with sin in the past. Do you minimize and ignore it, or are you motivated to confront and confess sin?

Faith in Action

Today's reading said, "Remember that you belong to Him completely; nothing else has the power to hold you captive." Write down a prayer below, asking God to help you deal with temptation and sin.

_____

_____

_____

_____

_____

Heavenly Father, I confess my recurring sins as offenses against You. Please cleanse them by the blood of Jesus. Remove my guilt, and let me realize I am forgiven and set free. Nothing has the power to hold me captive.

DAY 35

Confession and Forgiveness

Scripture Reading: 1 John 1:5–2:2   Key Verses: Colossians 2:13–14

You, being dead in your trespasses and the uncircumcision of your flesh, He has made alive together with Him, having forgiven you all trespasses, having wiped out the handwriting of requirements that was against us, which was contrary to us. And He has taken it out of the way, having nailed it to the cross.

What role does confession of sin play in the life of a believer? The answer to this question often swings to one of two extremes. Some say since Jesus is sufficient atonement for all our sin when we accept Him as Savior, confession of specific sins isn't necessary at all. Others believe a detailed confession is needed each time we sin in order for God to be motivated to continue to forgive us.

Neither idea views forgiveness from God's perspective. Colossians 2:13–14 (NASB) explains an essential truth: "When you were dead in your transgressions . . . He made you alive together with Him, having forgiven us all our transgressions . . . and He has taken it out of the way, having nailed it to the cross."

Jesus' blood covers all of your sins—past, present, and future. In confession, you agree with God that what you have done is sin, that it is absolutely wrong and not in accord with His plans.

He wants you to tell Him straightforwardly what you've done so that you can experience the power of His forgiveness. To restore your sense of fellowship with the Lord, confess the things that strain your relationship with Him. One by one, lay your sins at His feet and you will feel the burden lift from your heart.

Goals for the Day

- Read 1 John 1:5–2:2.
- Review the verses of the day, Colossians 2:13–14, and spend a few minutes thinking about how these words apply.

Faith in Action

Unconfessed sin will steal your peace. Spend a few moments confessing any known sin and asking God to forgive and restore you.

___

___

___

___

___

___

Father, thank You that the blood of Your Son, Jesus, covers all my sins—past, present, and future. One by one, I bring my sins to You. Lift their heavy burden from my heart.

DAY 36

A DONE DEAL

SCRIPTURE READING: Psalm 25   KEY VERSE: Isaiah 43:25

*I, even I, am He who blots out your transgressions for
My own sake; and I will not remember your sins.*

God never ridicules us or makes us feel unworthy. Instead, we read these words of Jesus:

"Just as the Father has loved Me, I have also loved you; abide in My love" (John 15:9 NASB).

"If you continue in My word, then you are truly disciples of Mine; and you will know *the truth, and the truth will make you free*" (John 8:31–32 NASB, *emphasis added*).

"I have called you friends, for all things that I have heard from My Father I have made known to you" (John 15:15 NASB).

Love and truth. God is love and the source of all truth. The love He has for you is the same love He has for His Son, the Lord Jesus Christ. He gives you this love through His grace and mercy. It is a pure love, not tainted by guilt or obligation.

Regardless of how deep your past transgression may be, God is near to free you with the truth of His Word. Nothing is stronger than His love. When He forgives, He forgets (Ps. 103:12; Isa. 43:25). Once you have confessed sin, there is no need to beg or plead for His forgiveness. It is a done deal!

You can walk freely in the light of His love because He calls you His child. Your life is inscribed within the palm of His hand.

You are the apple of His eye; all of heaven rejoices at the sight of your name written in the Lamb's Book of Life.

Goals for the Day

- Read Psalm 25.
- Glance back at the Scripture verses listed in today's reading. Which one most resonates with you right now?

Faith in Action

Today's reading said, "God is love and the source of all truth. The love He has for you is the same love He has for His Son, the Lord Jesus Christ." Write a prayer of thanks below, telling Him what this reality means to you.

O God, thank You for freeing me from sin with the power of Your Word. As I journey down life's road, let me walk freely in the light of Your love. Make me secure in my relationship with You.

DAY 37

The Slave Market of Sin

Scripture Reading: John 8:30–36   Key Verse: Galatians 5:13

You, brethren, have been called to liberty; only do not use liberty as an opportunity for the flesh, but through love serve one another.

Author Neil Anderson told of a time when he was talking to a group about living a bondage-free life. One man spoke up and told how he had enjoyed a certain activity most of his life without feeling a trace of bondage to it.

"I paused for a second," said Anderson, "then I said, 'Well, congratulations, but can you stop?'

"I didn't hear another remark from him again until the end of the class when everybody left. He came up and said, 'So why would I want to stop?'

"I said, 'That's not what I asked; I asked if you *could* stop. What you think is freedom really isn't freedom at all—it's bondage.'

"Anybody who acts as his own God is in bondage to his sinful nature. We were sold into the slave market of sin. Jesus purchased us from the kingdom of darkness and saved us from ourselves. We are not our own; we were bought at a very high price, the precious blood of Christ. We are no longer slaves to sin but servants to Christ."[1]

Many of us can relate to this story. Maybe your sin is gossiping. Or perhaps you have a difficult time telling the truth. You want people to think well of you, so you create stories that portray you in a heroic light.

Whatever the weakness, God can set you free. Ask Him to expose any sin in your life. Are you willing to give it up in order to live free?

Goals for the Day

- Read John 8:30–36.
- Review the key verse of the day, Galatians 5:13. Spend a few minutes thinking about how you would describe the meaning of this passage to a friend.

Faith in Action

Can you relate to the story from today's reading? If so, write down any habits, thoughts, or attitudes that have kept you in bondage. Get in the habit of confessing your sins daily and asking God for His forgiveness and deliverance.

_____

_____

_____

Lord, I want to live free! Take every bondage. Cleanse every sin. Expose every area of my life that needs change. I am willing to give up everything in order to live free.

DAY 38

"It Happened in the Spring"

Scripture Reading: 2 Samuel 11:1–5   Key Verse: Psalm 28:8

*The LORD is their strength, and He is the
saving refuge of His anointed.*

The following words may remind us of the beginning to a beautiful novel: "It happened in the spring, at the time when kings go out to battle..." However, the poetic beauty quickly erodes to tragedy when we read how David yielded to temptation. The danger that shouts to us is in thinking we are above reproach and could never fall as David did. No one is immune to sin. Only by keeping our spiritual walk before God pure are we given the strength to say no to temptation.

David could have turned and walked the other way. Instead, he stopped and allowed his eyes to gaze at something that would lead to ruin. The very fact that he had remained in Jerusalem when other kings were off at war lets us know that David had become soft and lazy. He sent his field commander into battle in his place, never stopping to think that the enemy was crouched at his side, waiting for a chance to strike.

If you are battling certain temptation, make a note of how David gave himself to sin. Ask God to show you how to avoid becoming lazy in your spiritual walk by taking advantage of the good things He provides. David had a sincere love for the Lord. Once he realized his sin, he turned from it and God restored him.

Goals for the Day

- Read 2 Samuel 11:1–5.
- Spend a few moments thinking about what stood out to you in today's reading.

Faith in Action

Today you read, "David had a sincere love for the Lord. Once he realized his sin, he turned from it and God restored him." Why is David's example the blueprint for repentance?

_____

_____

_____

_____

_____

_____

_____

_____

Precious Lord, I am not immune to sin. Help me keep my spiritual walk pure before You so that I have the strength to say no to temptation.

DAY 39

COMPLETE REDEMPTION

SCRIPTURE READING: 2 Samuel 12:1–23   KEY VERSE: Psalm 32:1

Blessed is he whose transgression is forgiven, whose sin is covered.

Once his sin was exposed, David was filled with remorse. Over the years he had enjoyed a close, personal relationship with God. When he found out that his fellowship with God was in jeopardy, he cried out, "I have sinned against the LORD" (2 Sam. 12:13 NASB). God forgave David, yet the consequences of his sin remained, and the child who was born as a result of his adultery with Bathsheba died.

Sin corrupts. It's like rust on a car; it eats into the finish and hides in hard-to-see places. Often when it is too late, the rust is exposed, but the car is ruined. David knew his only hope for restoration rested in God's forgiveness.

Psalm 32 is a beautiful testimony to God's cleansing touch in David's life. It also is a witness to us of God's mercy and unconditional forgiveness. No matter what you have done, God can and will forgive you when you repent. He promises to restore the years the locusts have eaten away—the years sin and disappointment devoured your purity (Joel 2:25).

In Isaiah 1:18, He tells us that He will make our sins as white as snow. Are you telling yourself that God can never use you because of something in your past? That is Satan's lie. God uses the broken things of this world to prove His redemption is complete and extended to all humanity.

Goals for the Day

- Read 2 Samuel 12:1–23.
- Think about this question from today's reading, "Are you telling yourself that God can never use you because of something in your past?" What are some ways you might have been tempted to believe this lie?

Faith in Action

David's repentance and remorse were evident in the psalms he wrote. How has your walk with God impacted the way you see the world?

_____

_____

_____

_____

_____

Dear heavenly Father, restore what the locusts have consumed—the years that sin and disappointment have devoured. You have a great plan for me, regardless of my past. I look with anticipation toward the future.

No matter what you have done, God can and will forgive you when you repent. He promises to restore the years the locusts have eaten away—the years sin and disappointment devoured your purity (Joel 2:25).

DAY 40

Freedom from Sin

Scripture Reading: 1 Samuel 15   Key Verses: Psalm 51:3–4

I acknowledge my transgressions, and my sin is always before me. Against You, You only, have I sinned, and done this evil in Your sight—that You may be found just when You speak, and blameless when You judge.

Saul deliberately disobeyed God, and even worse, he knowingly lied about it to the prophet Samuel. It was then that Samuel had to deliver the dreaded message that God had rejected Saul as king.

Was Saul sorry? Yes, but he never did accept full blame for his actions. You can hear the attempt at justification in his response: "I have sinned. I violated the Lord's command and your instructions. I was afraid of the men and so I gave in to them" (1 Sam. 15:24 NIV).

Now look at the words of King David, whom God appointed to be ruler after Saul. David had sinned grievously as well, but he said this: "I know my transgressions, and my sin is always before me. Against you, you only, have I sinned" (Ps. 51:3–4 NIV).

Can you tell the difference between these two confessions? Saul did not really repent, because he refused to acknowledge the sin as his own. But David knew better. He fully acknowledged his sin, asked God for forgiveness, and turned from his ungodly ways.

That is the kind of repentance God wants from you. He knows

your heart and your weaknesses, and He wants you to admit them and walk in His path for you. The Lord wants you to experience the relief and peace of being forgiven through Christ.

Goals for the Day

- Read 1 Samuel 15.
- Review the words David wrote in Psalm 51. Think about the differences between Saul's confession and David's.

Faith in Action

Write your own version of Psalm 51. Tell God how you've sinned, reveal any areas you feel remorseful, and ask Him to restore you.

_____

_____

_____

_____

_____

_____

_____

Master, I know my transgressions. My sin is always before me. Against You, and You only, have I sinned. I repent. Thank You for the blood of Jesus that cleanses my sin.

DAY 41

The Divine Scapegoat

Scripture Reading: Leviticus 16:1–22   Key Verse: Isaiah 53:6

All we like sheep have gone astray; we have turned, every one, to his own way; and the Lord has laid on Him the iniquity of us all.

Through repeated usage, the term *scapegoat* has become quite familiar to our secular culture. Its meaning—"an innocent party being blamed"—has its roots, however, in the ancient Hebrew festival known as the Day of Atonement.

This holy day occurred once each year. The high priest took two male goats as a sin offering for the iniquities of the people. One goat was slaughtered, and its blood was sprinkled on the mercy seat. The remaining goat was sent into the wilderness—after the high priest had placed his hands on the goat's head and confessed the sins of the nation over it. Through this "scapegoat" observance, God showed His mercy to the Israelites, allowing Him to continue His covenant relationship with them.

In much the same way, Jesus became the divine scapegoat for the sins of the world. He was and is the "Lamb of God who takes away the sin of the world!" (John 1:29 NASB).

Our sins were placed on Him at Calvary. Indeed, our sins put Him there. Jesus took the blame once and for all so that we could live. Have you trusted in His atonement? Have you come to Him for the forgiveness of your sins? Have you been healed of your transgressions through His sacrifice?

Goals for the Day

- Read Leviticus 16:1–22.
- Review the verse of the day, Isaiah 53:6. What stands out to you in this passage?

Faith in Action

Write your thoughts from today's lesson in the space below.

_____

_____

_____

_____

_____

_____

_____

_____

Almighty God, thank You for the sacrifice of Your Son, Jesus, as the divine scapegoat for my sins. I praise You that He took the blame so I could live. I rejoice in the liberating truth of His atonement for me.

DAY 42

Sensitivity to Sin

Scripture Reading: Numbers 22   Key Verse: Psalm 139:23

*Search me, O God, and know my heart;
try me, and know my anxieties.*

In Numbers 22, we read how Balak, the Moabite king, sought to persuade Balaam to prophesy against Israel by offering the pagan prophet a significant sum of money to curse God's chosen people.

God warned Balaam not to accept the offer. However, when Balak's men showed up at his door with an extra-large sum of cash, temptation won out. Balaam went back to God to see if there was a chance He had changed His mind. The Lord gave Balaam permission to go, but was angry at him for not heeding His first command.

God knows the true motivation of our hearts. Balaam told the men he would go with them but could say only what God told him to say. Here's the catch: Balaam wanted the money more than he wanted to do what was right. He knew God did not want him to go, but he was willing to risk everything in order to cash in on the situation.

Balaam's donkey was the only thing that saved him from God's wrath. She saw a mighty angel blocking their path and stopped. However, Balaam became so angry that he beat her.

The Spirit of God always reveals sin. However, we can choose to go against God's warning by compromising our convictions. When this happens, we suffer in our disobedience. Ask the Lord to make you sensitive to sin. Pledge your devotion to Christ, and He will guard your life.

Goals for the Day

- Read Numbers 22.
- Review the verse of the day, Psalm 139:23, and use it as a guide for your own prayer.

Faith in Action

Today's reading said, "Ask the Lord to make you sensitive to sin. Pledge your devotion to Christ, and He will guard your life." Are you willing? If so, write your own prayer saying so.

_____

_____

_____

_____

_____

_____

Dear God, make me sensitive to sin. Reveal the true motivations of my heart. I pledge my devotion to Christ. Let His power and truth guard me and direct my spiritual journey.

DAY 43

CONSEQUENCES OF COMPROMISE

Scripture Reading: Judges 2   Key Verses: Judges 2:1–2

The Angel of the Lord came up from Gilgal to Bochim, and said: "I led you up from Egypt and brought you to the land of which I swore to your fathers; and I said, 'I will never break My covenant with you. And you shall make no covenant with the inhabitants of this land; you shall tear down their altars.' But you have not obeyed My voice. Why have you done this?"

Peter Marshall once said, "We are too Christian really to enjoy sinning, and too fond of sinning to enjoy Christianity. Most of us know perfectly well what we ought to do; our trouble is that we do not want to do it."[1]

D. L. Moody wrote of a time when he had to stand for his personal convictions rather than be a part of compromise:

> Once I got into a place where I had to get up and leave. I was invited to a home, and they had a later supper, and there were seven kinds of liquor on the table. I am ashamed to say they were Christian people. A deacon urged a young lady to drink until her face was flushed. I rose from the table and went out; I felt that it was no place for me. They considered me very rude. That was going against the custom; that was entering a protest against such an infernal thing. Let us go against custom when it leads us astray.[2]

Some convictions are obvious because God outlines them in His Word. Others are personal between you and Him. Regardless, the principle remains the same. When God sets a warning in front of you, and you deliberately go against His command, you compromise your relationship with Him. God cannot bless disobedience or compromise. If you want His best, tell Him that wherever He leads, you will follow—forsaking all that does not bring glory and honor to Him.

Goals for the Day

- Read Judges 2.
- Spend a few minutes thinking about how disobedience and compromise keeps believers from experiencing God's best.

Faith in Action

Today's reading said, "God cannot bless disobedience or compromise." How would you describe the difference between disobedience and compromise? Why are both dangerous?

_____

_____

_____

*Lord, You cannot bless disobedience or compromise,
so I want to follow where You lead, forsaking all
that does not bring glory and honor to You.*

DAY 44

The Remedy for Sin

Scripture Reading: 2 Corinthians 5:14–21   Key Verse: Romans 8:1

*There is therefore now no condemnation to those
who are in Christ Jesus, who do not walk according
to the flesh, but according to the Spirit.*

D. L. Moody once said, "Looking at the wound of sin will never save anyone. What you must do is to look at the remedy."[3]

Worrying about temptation and past sins only leads to episodes of guilt. If you truly want to break the pattern of sin in your life, look to the cross of Jesus Christ. This is your only remedy for sin. It was where God displayed His unconditional love and forgiveness to all of mankind.

You may think what you have done in the past is too horrendous for God to forgive. But nothing can separate you from the love of God. His forgiveness and cleansing are for all who come to Him. You may be a believer who has given in to temptation; God wants to free you from this bondage. However, condemnation is not His way (Rom. 8:1).

He draws us to Himself through the gift of His love. He doesn't scold a person for doing wrong; He convicts them by showing them how their behavior is destroying their joy, identity, and contentment. God goes after the heart. The Word of God provides instruction on how to live a godly life; to this He adds His unconditional love. God knows once a person meets Jesus Christ, he is eternally changed and he needs help walking in his new life.

Goals for the Day

- Read 2 Corinthians 5:14–21.
- Write the key verse of the day, Romans 8:1, on a notecard or on your phone. Over the next few days commit it to memory.

Faith in Action

Take a few moments to think about Romans 8:1. Write down how you would paraphrase it in your own words below.

_____

_____

_____

_____

_____

_____

Precious heavenly Father, I look to the cross of Jesus Christ as the remedy for my sin. You displayed Your unconditional forgiveness there. Thank You for that precious sacrifice, the gift of Your love.

DAY 45

Sin Solution

SCRIPTURE READING: Galatians 6:4–9 KEY VERSE: Galatians 6:4

Let each one examine his own work, and then he will have rejoicing in himself alone, and not in another.

Can you get away with sin? You may cheat on a major school exam, pass the test and class, and do so without the teacher uncovering your deceit. You also may covertly engage in immoral behavior and falsely be perceived as morally upright.

The IRS may never catch your falsified income tax report. Your employer may never know you pilfered office supplies. But in each instance there are consequences for your actions. Even when others are unaware, God has established an inviolate moral law of sin and consequences. And although the consequences may be delayed, they will occur.

Paul applied the agrarian metaphor of sowing and reaping to our behavior. A crop is reaped much later than it is planted, but the harvest does come. Sooner or later, we experience the ramifications of our sin, since we are ultimately accountable to God.

Never underestimate the internal price you pay for sin. The weight of guilt is enormous. Bitterness and depression settle uncomfortably in your soul as you try to suppress the conviction of the Holy Spirit.

Confession and repentance are God's provisions—His solution—for dealing with transgression. Acknowledge yours to Him (and others when appropriate). Receive His forgiveness. You don't have to plead for it, just receive the gift of His pardon. Trust Him to help you handle the consequences.

Goals for the Day

- Read Galatians 6:4–9.
- Spend a few minutes in prayer giving thanks to God for His grace and goodness. Confess any sins and ask for His forgiveness.

Faith in Action

Today's reading said, "Confession and repentance are God's provisions—His solution—for dealing with trabnsgression." Why do you think confession and repentance are actually God's gift to us?

_____

_____

_____

_____

Father God, thank You for Your provisions of confession and repentance to deal with my sin. I acknowledge my sins and receive the gift of Your pardon. I trust You to handle the consequences of any bad spiritual seed I have sown in the past.

DAY 46

Consequences and Punishment

Scripture Reading: Hebrews 12:5–11   KEY Verses: Hebrews 12:5–6

You have forgotten the exhortation which speaks to you as to sons: "My son, do not despise the chastening of the Lord, nor be discouraged when you are rebuked by Him; for whom the Lord loves He chastens, and scourges every son whom He receives."

One great misconception about the nexus between sin and consequences is because of a distorted notion of the character and nature of God.

Too many people view God as a celestial law enforcement officer, seeking to apply strict punitive measures to our misbehavior. Such a God is certainly not meant to be enjoyed. This tragic conclusion exists because of the confusion between consequences and punishment. God has established the moral law of sin and consequence in the spiritual realm as surely as He has fixed the law of gravity in the temporal realm.

God has designed consequences for our behavior as a means to teach us wise, profitable behavior. When we err, the often unpleasant results of our actions help to prevent reoccurrence. Consequences are not punishment—they do not constitute retribution or revenge. On the contrary, God's penalty for sin was paid for by His Son at the cross, His justice and holiness both displayed and satisfied. He uses consequences as an expression of love to correct and keep us from evil.

Just as an earthly father uses consequences to teach his children, our heavenly Father allows the results of sin to instruct us in the ways of righteousness. His motivation is love, never punishment; and the consequences are always mingled with mercy.

Goals for the Day

- Read Hebrews 12:5–11.
- Think about a time when God brought consequences and discipline to your life. Did you get a glimpse of His mercy?

Faith in Action

Spend a few moments in prayer giving thanks to God for His mercy and kindness. Write down ways God has shown His mercy to you.

_____

_____

_____

_____

Dear Lord, thank You for consequences that teach me to walk in the way of righteousness. How grateful I am that Your motivation is love instead of punishment and Your judgments are mingled with mercy.

DAY 47

Shearing Suckers

Scripture Reading: John 15:1–8   Key Verse: John 15:5

I am the vine, you are the branches. He who abides in Me, and I in him, bears much fruit; for without Me you can do nothing.

Suckers are the small leafy offshoots on tomato plants. As harmless as they appear initially, they must be constantly pinched off from the main stems to produce healthy, abundant tomatoes. Permitted to grow, they divert the soil's nutrients into leaves and stems instead of fruit.

As Christ prunes your life, He carefully removes habits, addictions, misplaced priorities, and other extraneous matters that deplete your spiritual growth. Divinely schemed, the purging is executed so that the life of Christ might saturate your soul. The more God prunes, the more you experience the power of the Holy Spirit and bear His pleasant fruit.

Do you not want more of the life of Christ? More of His peace, joy, kindness, and patience? Do you not desire to be made like Him? Know that His pruning is for this sweeping purpose.

Never forget this fundamental factor—you have been placed into Christ by God, and He has been placed into your life through the habitation of the Holy Spirit. This is the significance of Christ's illustration of the Vine and the branches.

You are permanently and unalterably attached to the Vine. God's shears of loving care don't impair your fellowship with Christ. Instead, His using them is a sign of your vital union with the Vine, Jesus Christ. You belong to Him for eternity, and He has pledged Himself to constantly work for your good.

Goals for the Day

- Read John 15:1–8.
- Review the key verse of the day, John 15:5. What stands out to you in this passage?

Faith in Action

Spend a few moments thinking about the spiritual concept of abiding in Christ. How would you describe what it means to abide?

_____

_____

_____

_____

_____

Heavenly Father, take the divine shears of Your Word and trim the suckers from my life. Strengthen my union with the Vine and make me more productive spiritually.

DAY 48

SALVATION BRINGS PEACE

SCRIPTURE READING: 1 John 5:7–13   KEY VERSE: John 1:29

The next day John saw Jesus coming toward him, and said, "Behold! The Lamb of God who takes away the sin of the world!"

Being confident in your salvation is crucial to your peace. Have you ever wondered about your salvation? Many people do. They worry that they have done something to cause Jesus not to love them. They struggle with feelings of doubt, confusion, and fear. In 1 John 4:18 (NASB) we read, "There is no fear in love; but perfect love casts out fear, because fear involves punishment." The apostle John also reminded us that we are able to love God "because He first loved us" (v.19).

Even before you were born, God knew what you would look like—the color of your hair, the sound of your voice, and the successes and failures you would face. In spite of all you have or have not done, God continues to love you with an everlasting love.

Jesus came to earth with a clear goal in mind, and that was to save those who are lost. He never said, "Be perfect and receive My salvation." Salvation comes to us one way, by the grace of God. When we accept His Son in faith, we receive eternal life.

You can work a lifetime to be good and perfect and not be any closer to heaven than when you first started. Salvation is based not on your works but on the finished work of Jesus Christ at Calvary. He is the One who bore your sins—past, present, and future.

Goals for the Day

- Read 1 John 5:7–13.
- Give thanks to God for the work He has done, confess any sin that comes to mind, and accept His forgiveness and unconditional love as a blessing.

Faith in Action

Today you read, "Salvation is based not on your works but on the finished work of Jesus Christ at Calvary." How would you describe this spiritual truth to an unbeliever? Is there someone you need to share this truth with?

_____

_____

_____

_____

_____

O God, before I was born, You knew me. You knew my strengths and weaknesses, my successes and failures. Yet You love me with an unconditional, everlasting love. How I thank You!

DAY 49

The Precious Blood

Scripture Reading: 1 Peter 1:17–21   Key Verse: Romans 3:23

All have sinned and fall short of the glory of God.

In Genesis we read about God performing the first animal sacrifice: "The Lord God made garments of skin for Adam and his wife, and clothed them" (Gen. 3:21 NASB).

Adam Clarke writes it is not likely that "sacrifice could have ever occurred to the mind of man without an express revelation from God."[4] The slaying of the animals was His chosen way to atone for Adam and Eve's transgression. A blood sacrifice was the only payment that would suffice.

Many years later, God gave the Israelites specific commands concerning sacrifice for sins, from how to prepare the animal to what the priests should wear to what to do with the leftover portions from the altar. But the bottom-line requirement was still the same—blood.

When Jesus died on the cross, He literally took our place by becoming the ultimate and final sacrifice for mankind's sin. Once we accept Him as our Savior, our sins are covered by His precious, atoning blood.

Jesus submitted His life to the power of death for a time so that you can have life for all time. He satisfied once and for all God's requirement for forgiveness: "For the wages of sin is death, but the free gift of God is eternal life in Christ Jesus our Lord" (Rom. 6:23 NASB). The precious blood of Jesus is the only cleansing agent that works.

Goals for the Day

- Read 1 Peter 1:17–21.
- Glance back at the verse of the day, Romans 3:23, and spend a few moments pondering this reality.

Faith in Action

Today's reading said, "The precious blood of Jesus is the only cleansing agent that works." How does this truth motivate you to tell others about Jesus?

Lord, let the precious, cleansing blood of Your Son, Jesus, flow over my life today. O cleansing stream, cover me!

Jesus submitted His life to the power of death for a time so that you can have life for all time.

DAY 50

A Right View of Repentance

Scripture Reading: Luke 3:3–6   Key Verse: Matthew 3:2

[John the Baptist said,] "Repent, for the kingdom of heaven is at hand!"

When John the Baptist called out, "Repent, for the kingdom of heaven is at hand," some may not have realized he was preparing the way for the coming of the Messiah.

John had been selected to preach repentance so that when Christ came, the hearts and minds of the people would be open to the truth of God. Many who heard his message repented and turned from evil. Others considered him foolish and extreme.

Repentance and sincere devotion to Christ separate a person from the natural ways of the world. Many people need God's forgiveness, but they resist any involvement with Him that disrupts their present lifestyle.

True repentance is a humble, life-changing experience between you and God. It means you agree with the Lord that you are headed in the wrong direction. It involves a renewing of your mind and offers a new perspective on life—one of hope and lasting joy. Through repentance, we turn away from sin completely.

Paul urged his readers, "Do not be conformed to this world, but be transformed by the renewing of your mind" (Rom. 12:2 nasb). That was the same type of call John issued right before Jesus began His public ministry, and it is God's call to you today.

Goals for the Day

- Read Luke 3:3–6.
- Spend a few moments thinking about what true repentance looks like in the life of a Christ follower.

Faith in Action

Practically speaking, what are ways you can do as the apostle Paul instructed and "be transformed by the renewing your mind"? Write your thoughts below.

_____

_____

_____

_____

_____

_____

_____

Master, I answer Your call today. Adjust my moral and spiritual vision. Align my thinking with Yours. Renew my mind. Transform my life.

DAY 51

Division Among Believers

Scripture Reading: Colossians 3:1–17   Key Verse: Colossians 3:10

[You] have put on the new man who is renewed in knowledge according to the image of Him who created him.

Sin hurts and undercuts the body of Christ. Others feel the effects of a Christian's sin. The Christian worker who gossips at lunch and draws others into her conversation is guilty of slander. The sad result of her sin is that she tempts others to fall prey to her sin as well.

In an interview, evangelist E. V. Hill was asked what the greatest adversity is facing the body of Christ. Without hesitation, he replied that it is division among believers. The one group that has the knowledge to change the world for eternal good often ends up doing the most damage to its members.

Christians like to categorize sin; obvious things such as stealing, murder, and sexual misconduct are ranked high on the sin list. Yet "little" sins such as gossip and "white lies" are very seldom ranked. However, no sin escapes God's convicting hand, including feelings of unforgiveness, bitterness, anger, rage, malice, lying, slander, greed, idolatry, or immorality (Col. 3:5–10).

The apostle Paul told us to "put on the new self" and to be "renewed to a true knowledge according to the image of the One [Jesus Christ] who created [us]" (Col. 3:10 NASB). We are to be truthful, tender-hearted, and caring in our attitude toward others. Christ called us to love one another (John 13:34). Ask the Lord to reveal any sin you have in this area, and then claim His forgiveness by faith.

Goals for the Day

- Read Colossians 3:1–17.
- Write down anything that stood out to you in today's Bible reading.

Faith in Action

Practically speaking, what does it mean to do as the apostle Paul said, and "put on the new self"? How does that align with a life of purpose?

_____

_____

_____

_____

_____

_____

_____

Precious Lord, reveal any wrong attitudes I have toward others. Take any unforgiveness, bitterness, anger, rage, malice, lying, slander, greed, idolatry, or immorality out of my heart. Give me a pure love for others.

DAY 52

THE WAY TO LIFE

SCRIPTURE READING: Romans 14:7–12   KEY VERSE: Galatians 6:14

God forbid that I should boast except in the cross of our Lord Jesus Christ, by whom the world has been crucified to me, and I to the world.

Whenever we become tangled in sin, our first response should be one of grief and remorse, not just over what we have done but over whom we have hurt. When we say yes to sin, we grieve the heart of God.

When you are tempted to sin, ask yourself, *Who is the boss of my life?* If Jesus Christ is, then the desire to become involved with things that do not reflect God's nature usually fades and disappears over time.

Though each of us faces temptations periodically, saying no to sin should not be something we have to think over. Saying no is easy when you realize that saying yes hurts Someone whose love you can't live without.

Have you ever thought of God in this way—as Someone who loves you more than all the rest? Jesus came to demonstrate God's personal love to humanity. His death at Calvary said it all. He bore our sins out of love and eternal devotion.

Goals for the Day

- Read Romans 14:7–12.
- Spend your prayer time asking God to make you quick to repent from anything in your life that is unpleasing to Him.

Faith in Action

Today's reading said, "When you are tempted to sin, ask yourself, *Who is the boss of my life?*" Why is this an important step?

Dear heavenly Father, You are the divine Boss of my life. I say a resounding no to sin and an eternal yes to You. I choose to walk in the way of life.

DAY 53

The Transforming Grace of God

Scripture Reading: 1 Timothy 1:8–17   Key Verse: Ephesians 1:7

In Him we have redemption through His blood, the forgiveness of sins, according to the riches of His grace.

Concerned about her salvation, a woman met with her pastor. "I don't know how Jesus can accept me," she cried. "I want to give my life to Him, but I'm not ready. You don't know what I've done. Jesus can't possibly forgive me."

Feeling guilty about past wrongs is understandable. Sin is ugly in God's eyes, but He took care of the problem on the cross. When you agree with God that your sin is wrong and accept Jesus' payment in your place, you are freed by His blood—clean and righteous in God's sight. No one is too wicked, too horrible, too unlovable, or too vile for Jesus to love.

Paul, the missionary and apostle, said, "Christ Jesus came into the world to save sinners, among whom I am foremost of all. Yet for this reason I found mercy, so that in me as the foremost, Jesus Christ might demonstrate His perfect patience" (1 Tim. 1:15–16 NASB). One of the greatest evangelists of all time was once a vicious persecutor of Christians.

No matter what you have said or done, you can hold fast to this promise: "In Him [Jesus] we have redemption through His blood, the forgiveness of our trespasses, according to the riches of His grace" (Eph. 1:7 NASB).

Goals for the Day

- Read 1 Timothy 1:8–17.
- Review the key verse of the day, Ephesians 1:7.

Faith in Action

Living a life of purpose means embracing God's forgiveness and letting go of the past. Write down any areas where you struggle to embrace God's forgiveness. How does Ephesians 1:7 speak to your situation?

_____

_____

_____

_____

_____

_____

_____

O God, I claim it! In Christ I have redemption—through His blood—the forgiveness of my trespasses, according to the riches of His grace.

DAY 54

YOUR SIN IS FORGIVEN

Scripture Reading: Psalm 85   Key Verse: Psalm 85:2

You have forgiven the iniquity of Your people;
You have covered all their sin.

The store manager listened as the little girl explained how her mom had told her she could have only one toy car. However, not being able to choose between two, she stole the second one.

At home she tried to act surprised when two cars popped out of the same box, but her mom saw through her performance. Once her dad got home from work, the truth came out, and they returned to the store.

Looking up at the manager with tears in her eyes, the little girl told him she was sorry. Her dad paid for the item and placed it in his pocket. On their way home, she touched her father's hand and said, "Daddy, I'm sorry. I don't ever want to do that again."

He held her tiny hand in his and said, "Honey, that was a hard lesson for you to learn. But I hope you realize what happens when you do something wrong. I also want you to know your mom and I love you very much and so does God."

Once they were back home, he reached inside his pocket and tossed the toy in the trash. The little girl blinked in confusion. "Dad, why did you do that?"

"Because you're forgiven. Once you tell God you are sorry and receive His forgiveness, He'll never bring that sin up again and neither will I."

Goals for the Day

- Read Psalm 85.
- Write down any verses that stood out to you from your Bible reading.

Faith in Action

Write a prayer of thanks in the space below. Tell God all the reasons why you are grateful for His compassion and mercy.

_____

_____

_____

_____

_____

_____

Lord, I am so thankful that my sins are gone. You will never bring them up again. You have forgiven me; now help me to forgive myself.

DAY 55

A Casual View of Sin

SCRIPTURE READING: Romans 6:1–7   KEY VERSE: Romans 6:7

He who has died has been freed from sin.

Most of us have heard how a frog can be boiled to death without any resistance. Placed in a cool pot of water on a cooking surface, the frog remains content and unsuspecting as the heat beneath is increased. His internal temperature rises with the temperature of the water until finally he is boiled alive!

Abraham and Lot were given a choice about the land they would occupy. Lot, seeing the lushness of the Jordan Valley, chose the richness of Sodom, while Abraham settled in the land of Canaan.

Greed and lust fueled Lot's desires. F. B. Meyer wrote, "The younger man [Lot] chose according to the sight of his eyes. In his judgment he gained the world—but the world is full of Lots—shallow, impulsive, doomed to be revealed by their choice and end."[1]

Lot never considered the character of the inhabitants of the land. He adopted a casual view of their sin. And in doing so he failed to realize the effect of their presence on his relationship with God.

Have you adopted God's perspective on sin, or do you have an indifferent attitude toward what is unholy before holy God? Don't risk being lulled into deadly spiritual lethargy by the complacency of our society. God hates sin and calls us to do the same.

Goals for the Day

- Read Romans 6:1–7.
- Write down anything that stood out in today's Bible reading.

Faith in Action

Spend a few minutes thinking about ways you might be indifferent to sin. Ask God to reveal anything you need to change. Write your thoughts below.

_____

_____

_____

_____

_____

_____

_____

Father, I don't want to treat sin casually. Give me Your divine perspective on sin. Keep me from being lulled into spiritual lethargy by the complacency of the world in which I live. Let me understand—You hate sin, and You have called me to do the same.

DAY 56

Hazard of a Hard Heart

SCRIPTURE READING: Exodus 10   KEY VERSE: Exodus 8:19

The magicians said to Pharaoh, "This is the finger of God." But Pharaoh's heart grew hard, and he did not heed them, just as the LORD had said.

He had attended church since he was a small child. As an adult, he took careful notes on every sermon. When the pastor talked about specific sins, he recognized some of the problems in his own heart and said to himself, "That's me. I need to deal with these things." But like many, by the time he returned from church, he had forgotten about his plans to ask God to change his life.

The man has a hard heart. "How is that possible?" you may ask. "He's hearing what God says." When you hear God's Word and refuse to put it into practice, your heart is hardened against His truth. Eventually, if you continue to ignore His leading, He lets you follow your own slippery course.

God allowed Pharaoh to tell Moses no again and again. Pharaoh knew what he was supposed to do—release God's chosen people, the Israelites, from slavery and oppression. Because Pharaoh persisted in his disobedience, he learned painful lessons he could have avoided.

Ask God to sensitize your heart and make you aware of any tough spots of resistance. He will soften your spirit, renew your understanding, and set you on a course of true submission.

Goals for the Day

- Read Exodus 10.
- Spend your prayer time asking God to give you a tender heart toward Him.

Faith in Action

Take a quick spiritual inventory. Are you abiding in Christ and enjoying your relationship with Him? How is your prayer life? Are you obeying God's Word? Is there anything you need to change?

_____

_____

_____

_____

_____

_____

_____

Precious Lord, sensitize my heart. Make me aware of any hard spots of resistance. Soften my spirit, renew my understanding, and set me on a course of true submission.

DAY 57

Facing Failure

Scripture Reading: Luke 15:1–10   Key Verse: Luke 15:7

I say to you that likewise there will be more joy in heaven over one sinner who repents than over ninety-nine just persons who need no repentance.

The agony of the Christian life is not just sinning but trying our best to be godly and still failing. Once we know Christ, we want to please Him; we want to live in the light of His truth; we want to live victoriously. As a sage once said, "God didn't teach us how to swim in order to let us sink." God saved us so that we could enjoy and experience His abundant life. Yes, there are struggles, but we can win.

But how do we overcome the sins that constantly seem to overwhelm and subdue us? We must first come to the point of absolute repentance. How serious have we become about the sin that besets us? Do we see how offensive it is to God? Have we literally, completely changed our minds about it?

Genuine repentance is a deep, profound act. Most of us have not reached that level; we flirt with our sins. If we have repented, however, then step two is still essential—to recognize our new identity in Christ. Jesus indwells us with all of His might and divinity. We overcome through Him because He is the Overcomer. No sin can stand before Him as by faith we claim His total conquest gained at Calvary.

As we become serious about sin and recognize our new natures as believers, triumph is near.

Goals for the Day

- Read Luke 15:1–10.
- Spend a few moments thinking about why flirting with sin is counterproductive to God's plans for your life.

Faith in Action

Today's reading said, "As we become serious about sin and recognize our new natures as believers, triumph is near." Why are taking sin seriously and understanding our new natures two critical aspects of living a life of purpose and peace?

_____

_____

_____

_____

_____

Dear heavenly Father, I want to recognize and claim my new identity in You. Help me understand that Jesus dwells in me with all of His might and divinity. Let me realize that I can overcome through Him because He is the Overcomer.

DAY 58

God's Answer to Sin

Scripture Reading: John 3   Key Verse: John 3:3

Jesus answered and said to him, "Most assuredly, I say to you, unless one is born again, he cannot see the kingdom of God."

God's only answer to the problem of sin is Jesus Christ. No one can save himself; no person is "good" enough to get into heaven. One day each of us will stand before God and give an account of why He should allow us to enter His kingdom. What will your answer be?

Reasons such as being good and trying not to hurt anyone won't work. Jesus told Nicodemus, a man known for his extensive knowledge of the Jewish law and his sensitivity to spiritual matters, that he had to be born again to enter the kingdom of God (John 3:3). This "born again" phrase often evokes cynicism from nonbelievers, but God does not apologize for His Word.

The new birth Jesus talked about in John 3 is not physical but spiritual in nature. W. E. Vines explained, born again "is used metaphorically in the writings of the Apostle John, of the gracious act of God in conferring upon those who believe the nature and disposition of 'children,' imparting to them spiritual life."[2]

Only God's saving grace through a personal experience with Jesus Christ is the answer to humanity's sin. God does not want anyone to miss heaven's wonderful and perfect love. His greatest desire is that you would experience the love and forgiveness of His Son, the Lord Jesus Christ, for eternity. Have you placed your trust in Him?

Goals for the Day

- Read John 3.
- Is there someone you need to share the gospel with? Reach out to that person today.

Faith in Action

Write a prayer below asking for God's grace to envelop your unsaved friends and loved ones and help them receive the Good News of salvation through Jesus Christ.

_____

_____

_____

_____

_____

_____

Father God, I come Your way through Jesus Christ. Thank You for Your Answer to my sin. I place my eternal trust in Him.

DAY 59

Separated from Sin

Scripture Reading: Psalm 103　　KEY Verse: Psalm 103:13

As a father pities his children, so the Lord pities those who fear Him.

We read in Psalm 103:8–13 (nasb):

> *The Lord is compassionate and gracious,*
> *Slow to anger and abounding in lovingkindness.*
> *He will not always strive with us,*
> *Nor will He keep His anger forever.*
> *He has not dealt with us according to our sins,*
> *Nor rewarded us according to our iniquities.*
> *For as high as the heavens are above the earth,*
> *So great is His lovingkindness toward those who fear Him.*
> *As far as the east is from the west,*
> *So far has He removed our transgressions from us.*
> *Just as a father has compassion on his children,*
> *So the Lord has compassion on those who fear Him.*

Can you think of why it would be important to know that God has separated you from your sin? One answer is theologically based: Since God can have nothing to do with sin, He must completely remove sin from you through the blood of Jesus Christ in order to have a relationship with you.

Another reason is more subtle. If you do not grasp the fact that your sins are truly gone, then psychologically your sins are still hanging around. What happens when sin remains? You feel guilty, convicted, and unrighteous and these emotions can prevent you from living out God's purposes for your life. Positionally in Christ, your sin is gone; but this truth must be absorbed by you emotionally to be experientially real.

Goals for the Day

- Read Psalm 103.
- Use David's words from Psalm 103 to guide your prayer time.

Faith in Action

In your own words, write down what it means to have your sins removed "as far as the east is from the west."

_____

_____

_____

Father, thank You for separating me from my sin. It is not hanging around. It is not hiding. It is gone—removed as far as the east is from the west. Thank You!

Only God's saving grace

through a personal

experience with Jesus

Christ is the answer

to humanity's sin.

DAY 60

Behavior to Match Your Identity

Scripture Reading: 2 Corinthians 6:14–7:1 KEY Verse: 2 Corinthians 7:1

Therefore, having these promises, beloved, let us cleanse ourselves from all filthiness of the flesh and spirit, perfecting holiness in the fear of God.

An American on business in the Far East may not find it easy to assimilate into Asian culture. The food is different; there is a language barrier; the wardrobes are distinct. He is constantly reminded of the dissimilarities because his identity as an American is well established. He acts and thinks like an American precisely because he is one. Understanding your identity in Christ is even more important because it is pivotal for success in combating the world's influence. You must understand what no longer fits you as God's child.

A dramatic transformation occurred when you were saved. You became a "new creature" in Christ (2 Cor. 5:17 NASB). You became a citizen of God's kingdom. You still live in your indigenous culture, with all of its allures, trials, temptations, and charms; but you are no longer the same man or woman.

Living holy or separately from the impulses of the world is possible only as you realize the amazing metamorphosis that has transpired within. You are quite obviously still "in the world," but you are now not "of the world."

Learning who you are in Christ takes time, complete with failure, for your behavior to match your identity; but you have a lifelong, resident Teacher, the Holy Spirit, to help you along the way.

Goals for the Day

- Read 2 Corinthians 6:14–7:1.
- During your prayer time ask the Holy Spirit to help you so that your behavior matches your identity in Christ.

Faith in Action

In your own words, write down what it means to be "in the world" but not "of the world."

_____

_____

_____

_____

_____

Precious heavenly Father, You brought me out of the "Egypt" of sin and set my feet on the road to Your promised land. As I continue on this spiritual journey, help me match my behavior with my new identity.

DAY 61

BINDING BEHAVIORS

SCRIPTURE READING: 1 Peter 1:13–16   KEY VERSE: 1 Peter 1:13

Therefore gird up the loins of your mind, be sober, and rest your hope fully upon the grace that is to be brought to you at the revelation of Jesus Christ.

Here's how to handle binding behaviors that prevent you from living the life God intended for you. First, identify the problem. Be honest with yourself, or ask a trusted friend to be straightforward with you. Denying that you have a problem prevents you from experiencing true victory and hope.

Second, take responsibility for your behavior. No matter how small or large the habit may seem, admit that it exists and that you are responsible for its continued presence.

Third, trace the behavior to the source. Ask God to help you remember when you were programmed to feel or act a certain way. Low self-esteem, feelings of rejection, or helplessness all have beginning points. And these emotions lead to habits that weaken our ability to accept what Christ has done for us and can do through us.

Fourth, forgive yourself, and others who have hurt you. Forgiveness does not mean the person who hurt you can walk away without being punished. Forgiveness is something you do for yourself so that you can experience freedom from bitterness and resentment. God tells us that vengeance belongs to Him. Let the Lord have your hurt and pain, and He will take care of the situation.

Fifth, renew your mind with the truth of God's Word. When you do this, you will discover that God loves you more than you can imagine. You also will receive the needed strength and hope to be the person He created you to be.

Goals for the Day

- Read 1 Peter 1:13–16.
- From today's reading, review the five steps to address binding behavior.

Faith in Action

What habits and behavior do you need to apply the five steps of addressing binding behaviors to? Ask God to help you overcome.

_____

_____

_____

_____

Lord, I want to take responsibility for my own behavior. Reveal to me the reasons behind my negative responses, and then help me forgive myself and others. Heal my hurt and pain.

DAY 62

Journey to the Promised Land

Scripture Reading: Deuteronomy 11:1–17   Key Verse: Philippians 4:19

*My God shall supply all your need according
to His riches in glory by Christ Jesus.*

The nation of Israel had crossed the searing desert, battled numerous enemies, and wandered in the wilderness for forty years. Now—at last—they stood poised at the border of their promised land.

But there was a major problem. Jericho. A formidable walled city, it was a seemingly insurmountable obstacle that blocked their way.

Jericho was a divinely planned impediment in the life of Israel. The outcome of the battle would bring glory to God and provide conclusive evidence to Israel that He was doing exactly what He had promised He would do.

As you follow Christ, you, too, will experience your own Jerichos. Oftentimes when God calls you to do something, you'll experience a barrier that threatens your progress. Don't be surprised by them—come to expect them. God's Word teaches readers to recognize obstacles in your journey of faith as opportunities to discover your true identity in Christ and to tap into His sufficiency. By depending on Christ's power to confront the hurdles on your path, you'll learn to walk by faith and not by sight.

Goals for the Day

- Read Deuteronomy 11:1–17.
- Jericho was blocking the Israelites entry into the promised land. Identify any obstacles that are blocking you from the life God wants you to have.

Faith in Action

Today's reading said, "God's Word teaches readers to recognize obstacles in your journey of faith as opportunities to discover your true identity in Christ and to tap into His sufficiency." How does this truth apply to your challenges?

_____

_____

_____

_____

_____

_____

Lord, I pray for the faith to confront my Jerichos in your power. Give me the courage I need to move forward in faith.

DAY 63

OBSTACLES OR OPPORTUNITIES?

Scripture Reading: Deuteronomy 11:18–28   Key Verse: Deuteronomy 11:26

Behold, I set before you today a blessing and a curse.

Joshua and the nation of Israel were preparing to enter the promised land. Moses would not go with them. His last responsibility as their leader would be to issue a charge concerning the land they were about to enter. Moses explained that if they would keep the commandments of the Law, then God would drive out their enemies before them.

Often we find ourselves wondering why God does not remove all the obstacles after He blesses us. The excitement of a new job turns sour the moment we find out the boss has a dark side. The dream house becomes a nightmare when we find out the roof leaks and the water heater needs replacing.

Many times God places such impediments in our lives to keep us humble and dependent on Him. The very name God gave the promised land—Canaan—means "a place of humility." The Israelites longed to enter the land of their inheritance, yet they realized that along with the promise came the tests and trials of life.

There will be times when you feel as though you have run into a brick wall. The obstacles facing you may seem overwhelming, but take heart. These are the times God wants you to turn to Him and trust Him to remove the barriers blocking your path.

Goals for the Day

- Read Deuteronomy 11:18–28.
- Spend your prayer time asking God for wisdom to deal with the obstacles you are facing.

Faith in Action

Today's reading said, "Many times God places such impediments in our lives to keep us humble and dependent on Him." With this in mind, how can obstacles actually turn out to be a blessing?

_____

_____

_____

_____

_____

_____

_____

Dear Lord, when it seems that a brick wall looms ahead, let me turn to You. Help me realize that obstacles keep me dependent on Your power. I trust You to remove every barrier from my path in Your perfect timing.

DAY 64

FACING THE JERICHOS OF LIFE

SCRIPTURE READING: Joshua 6   KEY VERSE: Joshua 1:6

*Be strong and of good courage, for to this people
you shall divide as an inheritance the land which
I swore to their fathers to give them.*

No military officer worth his stripes would go into conflict unprepared, without a clear and cogent plan of attack. The risk would be too great, and the chances of winning slim. Yet that was exactly what God wanted Joshua to do—approach the awesome, fortified city of Jericho without the first conventional military procedure. Literally all God gave to Joshua were his marching orders and the promise that the Israelites would be the winners.

How could Joshua hold his head high and approach the battlefield with confidence? He knew who was in charge. He did not have to worry about defeat or loss. Any momentary feelings of weakness came crashing down with the walls and were forgotten in the glory of taking the city for the Lord.

When you face a Jericho in your life—a problem you cannot solve or the seemingly impenetrable fortress of a broken relationship—trust God for the conquest. Obey His Word and apply His principles to each situation.

You may not understand how the sequence of events will unfold, and you may not feel the emotion of triumph while you wait for the outcome. But in the Lord you cannot lose; the victory is yours.

Goals for the Day

- Read Joshua 6.
- Spend your prayer time asking God to increase your trust in Him.

Faith in Action

Today's reading instructed you to: "obey His Word and apply His principles to each situation." Write down the next steps you need to take.

_____

_____

_____

_____

_____

_____

Heavenly Father, as I face the Jerichos of life, give me assurance that victory is mine. I want to respond to Your marching orders and not worry about the seemingly impenetrable fortresses ahead.

DAY 65

CHARACTERISTICS OF TRUE BELIEVERS

Scripture Reading: Ephesians 1:1–14   Key Verse: Ephesians 1:11

In Him also we have obtained an inheritance, being predestined according to the purpose of Him who works all things according to the counsel of His will.

A life of enduring holiness (reflecting the mind and character of God) is possible only when we first are convinced of our identity in Christ. Scripture attributes these remarkable characteristics to believers:

- We are the salt of the earth.
- We are saints.
- We are joint heirs with Jesus.
- We are justified by faith.
- We are ambassadors for Christ.
- We are eternally secure in Christ.
- We are triumphant in Christ.
- We are accepted in the Beloved.
- We are children of God.
- We have peace with God.
- We are free from condemnation.
- We are the temple of God.
- We are blessed with every spiritual blessing.
- We are citizens of heaven.
- We are complete in Christ.

Many other blessings are already yours through faith in Christ as well. They are gifts from the Father, bestowed upon every disciple for effective service.

Knowing who you are in Jesus is the starting point for abundant living. You can live a holy life because you are righteous in Christ. Today agree with God concerning your new identity in Him.

Goals for the Day

- Read Ephesians 1:1–14.
- Review the list from today's reading. Which of these characteristics stand out to you?

Faith in Action

Give thanks to God for your identity in Christ. Praise Him for the characteristics from today's reading that are especially meaningful to you.

O God, I declare my new identity in Christ: I am the salt of the earth, a child of God, a saint who has peace with You. I am joint heir with Jesus, free from condemnation, and justified by faith. I am the temple of God, an ambassador for Christ, eternally secure, triumphant, complete, and accepted in Christ. I am a citizen of heaven and blessed with every spiritual blessing!

DAY 66

THE SUFFICIENCY OF CHRIST

Scripture Reading: Ephesians 1:15–23   Key Verse: Colossians 1:18

*He is the head of the body, the church, who is the
beginning, the firstborn from the dead, that in
all things He may have the preeminence.*

As Paul addressed the deity and power of Christ in the first chapter of Colossians, he continually stressed the preeminence of Christ. Paul said He is "the firstborn of all creation," "the firstborn from the dead," and the One who is "to have first place in everything" (vv. 15, 18 NASB).

Paul's use of the term *first place* was not, however, the comparative term we sometimes imagine. He was not saying that Jesus is prominent—that is, Christ is first, my family second, the church third, my job fourth, and so on. That wasn't Paul's or God's intention.

What Paul—and the Spirit who inspired him—was attempting to communicate was that Jesus is preeminent. Jesus is above and beyond anyone and anything. Jesus is to be first in our homes, first in our finances, first in our relationships, first in our jobs, first in our leisure time, first and foremost in every conceivable aspect of life. Nothing can compare to Christ. He came not to be on the top of a priority list but to fill all with His fullness.

Is Christ the undisputed Lord over all of your life, reigning supreme? Have you allowed Him "to have first place in everything"?

Goals for the Day

- Read Ephesians 1:15–23.
- Review the verse of the day. Think about how you would describe the preeminence of Christ to a curious friend.

Faith in Action

Write down your thoughts on what it looks like when Jesus is first in every aspect of your life.

_____

_____

_____

_____

_____

_____

_____

_____

Jesus, You are above and beyond anyone or anything in my life. You are first in my home, my finances, my relationships, my leisure time, and my work. You are undisputed Lord over my life.

DAY 67

UNCHANGING JOY

Scripture Reading: John 6:32–40   Key Verse: John 6:40

This is the will of Him who sent Me, that everyone who sees the Son and believes in Him may have everlasting life; and I will raise him up at the last day.

Although the Christian life is most certainly a fight of faith, it is not endless striving and straining. There is a monumental difference between abiding in Christ and striving, and understanding the dissimilarity can majorly affect how much joy, peace, and contentment we experience as we serve Christ.

J. Hudson Taylor, the founder of China Inland Mission, wrestled with the distinction until one day, at age thirty-seven, he saw the total sufficiency of Christ for every need. The catalyst for this liberating discovery was a personal letter from a missionary friend, John McCarthy, who wrote,

> To let my loving Savior work in me His will, my sanctification is what I would live for by His grace. Abiding, not striving nor struggling; looking off unto Him ... to subdue all inward corruption; resting in the love of an Almighty Savior ... This is not new and yet 'tis *new to me*. I feel as though the first dawning of a glorious day had risen upon me. I hail it with trembling and yet with trust.

I seem to have got to the edge only, but of a sea which is boundless; to have sipped only, but of that which fully satisfies.

Christ literally all seems to me now the power, the *only* power for service; the only ground for unchanging joy.[1]

Goals for the Day

- Read John 6:32–40.
- Spend a few moments doing a spiritual inventory. Are you abiding or striving?

Faith in Action

Describe the difference between striving and abiding. What are some characteristics of each?

_____

_____

_____

_____

_____

_____

_____

Lord, help me abide in You and not struggle or strive. You are my power for service, my only ground for unchanging joy.

DAY 68

Christ in You

Scripture Reading: John 14:15–27   Key Verse: John 16:14

He will glorify Me, for He will take of what is Mine and declare it to you.

How does God Himself, whose immensity cannot be measured, reside in such frail bodies as ours? How does the transcendent Christ live in finite human temples?

We may not comprehend the vastness of this principle, yet the method by which God imparts His presence is plain and clear in Scripture: Christ lives in us through His indwelling Holy Spirit. The Holy Spirit supernaturally brings the reality of Christ into our earthly frames.

As the third person of the Trinity, the Holy Spirit is just as much deity as the Father and the Son. He imparts the life of Christ to us through His residence in our lives.

The Holy Spirit reveals and shares with us all that Jesus is. By making His home in us, He assures us of the presence and power of the risen Christ.

Because the Holy Spirit possesses all the attributes of deity and because He inhabits our mortal bodies, He is infinitely adequate to meet any of our needs. He is not God far off but God who is near.

The resurrected Christ is your sure and steadfast hope for all of life, a hope that is every believer's to claim because of the indwelling ministry of the Holy Spirit.

Goals for the Day

- Read John 14:15–27.
- Today's reading said, "He is not God far off but God who is near." Let this truth guide your prayer time.

Faith in Action

Write your thoughts from today's reading below.

___

Come, Holy Spirit, and do Your work. Reveal all that Christ is and wants to be to me. Give me assurance of His presence and power. Let the same Spirit who raised Christ from the dead work abundantly in me.

DAY 69

THE WISDOM OF GOD

SCRIPTURE READING: Proverbs 1:1–7   KEY VERSE: Proverbs 1:7

*The fear of the LORD is the beginning of knowledge,
but fools despise wisdom and instruction.*

The apostle Paul made a clear distinction between the learned knowledge of his time and the wisdom of God. Such a difference still exists in this so-called intellectual age. As we send men into space and harness the atom, we still must be sure to lock our doors at night.

The wisdom of God is as superior to the insight of men as a star is to a sixty-watt bulb. Man's wisdom is based on limited knowledge and the utilization of discoverable data. God's wisdom is fathomless and perfect—providing strength, guidance, and the right course for every person in every age in every circumstance.

Perhaps the best definition of *wisdom* is "viewing life from God's perspective." That means sifting our ambitions, challenges, problems, and tasks through the filter of God's eternal truth—Scripture.

God's wisdom can never be achieved through a mechanical formula. If that were the case, then any person—wicked or righteous—could enjoy its benefits. Receiving God's wisdom involves developing a growing, intimate relationship with Jesus Christ, who is our wisdom (1 Cor. 1:30).

That's what Solomon meant when he said, "The fear of the LORD is the beginning of knowledge" (Prov. 1:7). As we seek and worship God and submit to His will, we increasingly become the repository of His wisdom.

Goals for the Day

- Read Proverbs 1:1–7.
- Write the verse of the day on a notecard or on your phone. Commit it to memory.

Faith in Action

Write a prayer below asking God to increase your wisdom.

_____

_____

_____

_____

_____

_____

_____

Precious Lord, let me view life from Your perspective. Help me sift my ambitions, challenges, problems, and tasks through the filter of Your truth. Give me divine wisdom through an intimate relationship with Your Son, Jesus.

Perhaps the best definition of *wisdom* is "viewing life from God's perspective." That means sifting our ambitions, challenges, problems, and tasks through the filter of God's eternal truth—Scripture.

DAY 70

Prevailing Peace

Scripture Reading: John 15:18–25   Key Verse: 2 Thessalonians 3:16

Now may the Lord of peace Himself give you peace always in every way. The Lord be with you all.

Europe trembled. Hitler's menacing armies were poised for a strike against Poland. Attempting to appease the dreaded dictator, England's prime minister, Neville Chamberlain, traveled to Germany and, on September 29, 1938, signed the infamous Munich Pact. Upon his return Chamberlain triumphantly announced, "I believe it is peace for our time."[2] A short time later Germany violated the treaty, invaded Poland, and World War II began.

Was Jesus' talk of peace like Chamberlain's optimistic boast? After all, why talk of such when war, violence, greed, and ill will still abound? Although Jesus taught much about peace and promised the disciples (and us) that He would leave us His peace, He did not ignore the reality of the world's conflict.

That's why His Passover message concerning peace was immediately followed by this clarification: "In the world you will have tribulation" (John 16:33). Jesus was a realist. There is nothing of evasiveness or idealism in His ministry. How, then, could He promise peace?

Christ Himself is our peace. His presence, strength, and comfort are ours in every gale—for He is always with us.

Goals for the Day

- Read John 15:18–25.
- Review the verse of the day and let it guide your prayer time.

Faith in Action

Write down any new insights or things that stood out to you from today's reading.

_____

_____

_____

_____

_____

_____

_____

_____

_____

Dear heavenly Father, thank You that despite the tribulation in this world, I can have peace. I claim Christ as my peace right now. I accept His presence, strength, and comfort as I face the storms of life.

DAY 71

Genuine Security

Scripture Reading: James 4:13–14   Key Verse: Proverbs 27:1

*Do not boast about tomorrow, for you do not
know what a day may bring forth.*

The older we grow, the more security conscious we may become. The prospects of putting kids through college and providing for retirement, savings, and investments take on disproportionate significance.

In reality, however, our sense of well-being is never assured by earthly means. Economic collapse, sickness, political or environmental fluctuations, or any number of unknown factors could seriously jeopardize our best-laid plans.

That is possible at any stage of life. That is the disquieting point of Proverbs 27:1: "Do not boast about tomorrow, for you do not know what a day may bring forth."

Our only genuine security lies in our relationship with Jesus Christ. That is universally applicable because God is sovereign, which means that God is in control. The *New Bible Dictionary* explains He "guides and governs all events, circumstances, and free acts of angels and men . . . and directs everything to its appointed goal for His own glory."[1] Your security lies in His power to work everything for your good and His glory.

That is also eternally relevant because God is immutable. That means God is always the same and operates on unchanging principles.

Goals for the Day

- Read James 4:13–14.
- During your prayer time give thanks to God for being your constant source of stability.

Faith in Action

Today's reading said, "Your security lies in His power to work everything for your good and His glory." Write down specific situations in your life that this truth applies to.

_____

_____

_____

_____

_____

Almighty God, I praise You that every detail of my life is directed by Your sovereign hand. I rest in the assurance that You govern each event and circumstance. I am secure in the knowledge that Your power weaves the dark and rough threads of life into a pattern for my good and Your glory.

DAY 72

Amazing Grace

Scripture Reading: Ephesians 2:1–10.   Key Verse: Ephesians 2:13

Now in Christ Jesus you who once were far off have been brought near by the blood of Christ.

It is little wonder that the hymn "Amazing Grace" is sung so resoundingly in churches across the world. Its vivid imagery reminds us of the preeminence of grace and its indispensable role in our salvation and sanctification. But what makes grace so amazing?

God's grace is amazing because it is free. No currency exists that can ever purchase grace. We are usually suspicious of anything free, but God's offer is without any hidden strings. He bore the cost for our sins (therefore, it is not cheap grace) so that He could extend it freely to any person on the basis of faith—not intellect, status, or prestige.

God's grace is amazing because it is limitless. His grace can never be exhausted. Regardless of the vileness or number of our sins, God's grace is always sufficient. It can never be depleted; it can never be measured. He always gives His grace in fullness.

God's grace is amazing because it is always applicable. Do you need wisdom? God's grace provides it through His Word. Do you need strength or guidance? God's grace sustains you by His Spirit. Do you need security? God's grace supplies it through His sovereignty.

The amazing grace of God! Full and free! Without measure! Pertinent for your every need!

Goals for the Day

- Read Ephesians 2:1–10.
- Identify areas where you need God's grace. Spend your prayer time asking God to pour out His grace on your life.

Faith in Action

Write down any thoughts and insight from today's reading. What does God's grace mean to you personally?

_____

_____

_____

_____

_____

_____

It's free! It's limitless! It is applicable to my every need today! O Lord, thank You for Your amazing grace. I praise You that it flows full and free in my life.

DAY 73

SUPERNATURAL STRENGTH

SCRIPTURE READING: Hebrews 12:1–3   KEY VERSE: 1 Peter 5:7

Casting all your care upon Him, for He cares for you.

Spiritual fatigue hits everyone. In the race to know and serve Christ, our bodies, minds, and hearts can reach an overload point, causing us to drop back. If severe enough, spiritual fatigue can discourage us from future participation.

God's strength to endure is ours when we "lay aside every encumbrance, and the sin which so easily entangles us" (Heb. 12:1 NASB). Cast your burdens on the Lord (1 Peter 5:7). Keep short accounts with God daily concerning your sin.

God's strength comes when we recognize that "in due time we will reap if we do not grow weary" (Gal. 6:9 NASB). Your efforts will pay off. Harvesttime will come. Your toil will be rewarded. God promises it.

God's strength comes to finish the race when we are not "worried about tomorrow; for tomorrow will care for itself" (Matt. 6:34 NASB). Live one day at a time. Do not be unduly concerned about tomorrow. The race is run step-by-step. So rest when He shows you it is time to cease your labors (Ps. 127:2).

God's strength comes when we let Him turn our weaknesses into His strengths: "He gives strength to the weary, and to him who lacks might He increases power" (Isa. 40:29 NASB).

When you are weary, draw from almighty God's unlimited power supply. Faint not. Fear not. Fret not. He gives supernatural strength to finish the race.

Goals for the Day

- Read Hebrews 12:1–3.
- Use the verse of the day, 1 Peter 5:7, to guide your prayer time.

Faith in Action

Practically speaking, what does it look like for you to "cast your cares on the Lord"?

_____

_____

_____

_____

_____

_____

_____

Dear God, transform my human weakness into supernatural strength. Let me faint not, fear not, and fret not. Give me supernatural strength to finish the race.

DAY 74

The Cycle of Blessing

Scripture Reading: Psalm 145   Key Verse: Proverbs 10:22

*The blessing of the Lord makes one rich,
and He adds no sorrow with it.*

Nature's cyclical pattern marks God's scheme of blessing. All blessings come from above (Gen. 49:25; Eph. 1:3). As Creator of all, the Lord is the Giver of life along with what sustains us (Ps. 145:15–16).

Heat from the sun, moisture from the rains, and oxygen in the atmosphere originated in His mind and exist through His wisdom and power (Gen. 1:1–2:3). He is the Designer of our bodies—organs, bones, tissues, muscles, nerves.

Our Father is also the Originator of our spiritual blessings. We can know God only because He first chose to reveal Himself through His creation; His Son, our Lord Jesus Christ; and the Bible (1 John 4:19).

When we receive the blessings of God through faith, the cycle continues as we share His presence in our conversation and our deeds. God told Abraham: "I will bless you ... and so you shall be a blessing" (Gen. 12:2 nasb).

The Lord favors us with His encouragement, hope, and joy. In turn we encourage the fainthearted, revive the sagging soul, and bring cheer to the afflicted.

Are you participating in God's cycle of blessing? Look to Him as your Resource; then look to help others.

Goals for the Day

- Read Psalm 145.
- Use Psalm 145 as a guide for your prayer time.

Faith in Action

In Psalm 145, David praises God. Write down several reasons that God is worthy of your praise.

___

___

___

___

___

___

___

Precious heavenly Father, You are the Originator of all my spiritual blessings. Help me to plug into Your divine cycle of blessing. Let me look to You as my divine Resource in every situation, and then reveal ways I can bless others.

DAY 75

How to Count Your Blessings

Scripture Reading: Psalm 34   Key Verse: Psalm 34:8

Oh, taste and see that the Lord is good; blessed is the man who trusts in Him!

When you are asked to count your blessings, your list may not be overwhelming. You may struggle to make ends meet; your days may be challenging. You are grateful for much, but weariness clouds your vision.

Pause to think of this: When you have the Lord Jesus Christ, you have the greatest blessing possible. That is not spiritualizing; it is the bedrock of your existence now on earth and one day in heaven.

In Christ you have the guarantee of eternal life. Life here may be unsettling, but a place of unparalleled beauty and joy awaits the one who knows Christ as Savior, Lord, and Life. Heaven is real, and its blessings are sure.

In Christ Jesus you have the Source of true life. He gives love, joy, peace, strength, comfort, hope, and patience. He nourishes your soul and energizes your spirit. Possessions are nice, but they cannot impart life—only Jesus can.

In Christ you have a Friend for all seasons. He understands your disappointments, rejoices in your triumphs, and stands with you in your trials. You can confide in Him, weep before Him, and celebrate with Him.

Begin with all you have in Jesus Christ when you count your blessings. Then you will lose count.

Goals for the Day

- Read Psalm 34.
- Use Psalm 34 as a guide for your prayer time.

Faith in Action

David wrote, "I will bless the LORD at all times. His praise will always be on my lips" (Ps. 34:1). Write down several things you are grateful to God for.

_____

_____

_____

_____

_____

Jesus, You are my greatest Source of blessing. You are my life. You give love, joy, peace, strength, comfort, and hope. You nourish my soul and energize my spirit. Thank You, Lord!

DAY 76

Clothed with Power

Scripture Reading: Luke 24:44–49   Key Verse: John 6:63

It is the Spirit who gives life; the flesh profits nothing. The words that I speak to you are spirit, and they are life.

After Jesus rose from the dead and ascended to the Father, His disciples were zealous to spread His message of salvation. Yet Christ commanded them to wait until they were "clothed with power from on high" (Luke 24:49 NASB) on Pentecost when the Holy Spirit would come for a new, indwelling ministry.

Think seriously about this fact: If the Holy Spirit was necessary for the apostles to live and minister effectively, do we not need His power as well? The Christian life is started by the Holy Spirit in the new-birth experience and continued by the same Holy Spirit.

We need God's Holy Spirit to enable us to live in victory over our circumstances. Only He gives us His hope, strength, and peace in the midst of crises. Only He supplies the mind and life of Christ when our emotions and situations are unpredictable and unstable.

We need the Holy Spirit to carry out the commands of Scripture through us. We can love our enemies, give thanks in heartache, deny ourselves, and turn the other cheek when we are ridiculed—only as He expresses Christ's life through us.

The Lord gives you His all-sufficient Holy Spirit to glorify Himself through you. Let Him complete what He started in you at salvation by yielding to His reign daily.

Goals for the Day

- Read Luke 24:44–49.
- Refer back to the verse of the day, John 6:63. Circle any words or phrases that stand out to you in this passage.

Faith in Action

Ponder this from today's reading: "If the Holy Spirit was necessary for the apostles to live and minister effectively, do we not need His power as well?" Write your thoughts below.

Dear Lord, I yield to Your reign in my life so that You can complete what You started in me at salvation. Enable me to live in victory over my circumstances. Give me the mind of Christ when my emotions and situations are unstable.

DAY 77

A Changed Life

Scripture Reading: John 3:1–17   Key Verse: Psalm 62:1

Truly my soul silently waits for God; from Him comes my salvation.

After we are saved, the constant pressure to conform to the world's standards can give us spiritual amnesia. We have to pay the electric bill on time, fight the rush-hour traffic, mow the yard, and wash the dishes just as everyone else does. The danger is that the familiar routine can cause us to lose sight of the radical transformation that occurred when we were born again.

At salvation, we received a new spirit, the Holy Spirit, who works through our ordinary experiences to accomplish the supernatural goal of conforming us to the image of Christ. In our bill paying, we can depend on His provision. In the irritating traffic snarls, we can meditate on Scripture. (Try it, it works!) In the yard work, we can enjoy His creation. In the kitchen, we can give thanks for His many gifts to us.

As new creatures with a new spirit, we have a new purpose—to honor God in all we do: working, eating, drinking, driving, playing, and thinking.

If your Christian experience borders on boring, remember the monumental change that occurred when you were saved and the divine dimension that is now yours to enjoy by faith and obedience.

Goals for the Day

- Read John 3:1–17.
- Using the verse of the day, Psalm 62:1, as a guide, spend a few moments sitting silently before God giving thanks for your salvation.

Faith in Action

What are some of the changes that have taken place in you since you became a Christian? Write your thoughts below.

_____

_____

_____

_____

_____

_____

_____

Heavenly Father, thank You for the tremendous change that occurred when I was saved. Thank You for the divine dimension that is mine to enjoy in every area of my life. I want to honor You in all I do.

DAY 78

God's Workmanship

Scripture Reading: Matthew 22:34–40   Key Verse: Matthew 22:40

On these two commandments hang all the Law and the Prophets.

Some evangelicals espouse the warped view that loving ourselves is selfish and wrong. While Christians obviously are called to love God and others, loving ourselves in a biblical, non-narcissistic fashion fosters a healthy spiritual balance. We love ourselves properly when we see ourselves as God sees us.

God declares His children to be His workmanship. He views us as men and women of inestimable worth—valuable enough to give His own Son on our behalf.

Your clothes, home, car, work, and friends do not determine your worth. God does. He values you so much that He desires to spend eternity with you.

We also love ourselves rightly when we treat ourselves properly. As God's masterpieces, we should take care of ourselves. Our bodies need balanced nutrition and exercise. Our personal grooming should be neat. We polish our furniture and wax our cars because they are objects of worth to us. Are we not worth more than they?

You are God's good and lovely creation. The more you affirm God's evaluation of yourself, the more you will adore Him and love others.

Goals for the Day

- Read Matthew 22:34–40.
- Spend your prayer time asking God to help you see your worth from His perspective.

Faith in Action

Today's reading said, "Your clothes, home, car, work, and friends do not determine your worth. God does." How does this truth impact the way you see yourself?

_____

_____

_____

_____

_____

_____

_____

_____

O God, You have declared me to be of inestimable worth. Help me view myself as You see me—valuable enough to give Your own Son on my behalf.

DAY 79

Your True Identity

SCRIPTURE READING: Ephesians 4:17–24   KEY VERSE: Ephesians 4:24

You put on the new man which was created according to God, in true righteousness and holiness.

Determining identity is a lifelong struggle for many people. Teenagers look to peers and parents trying to discover their unique identity. Possessions and status are often the criteria for the majority of their conclusions. Adults tend to define their identity by their vocation, financial bracket, or social strata. Determining our identity greatly affects our behavior. We act like who we think we are.

One of the greatest assets of the Christian is that his identity is rooted in the person of Jesus Christ. Because he is a child of God—an heir of God, a citizen of heaven as well as earth, a saint, and God's workmanship—he can act accordingly.

Do you know who you are in Christ?

Your marriage, career, relationships, and ambitions all hinge upon your new relationship with God's Son, Christ Jesus.

Your values, priorities, and perspectives are determined by this new relationship with Jesus. You are secure in Him. You are complete in Him. Your past, present, and future are bound up in the person of Jesus Christ.

Goals for the Day

- Read Ephesians 4:17–24.
- Take some time to think more deeply about this truth: "One of the greatest assets of the Christian is that his identity is rooted in the person of Jesus Christ."

Faith in Action

Write down any new insights that stood out to you in today's reading.

Father, I am thankful that I am complete in Your Son, Jesus Christ. My past, present, and future are bound up in Him. Let my values, priorities, and perspectives always reflect this divine relationship.

———

One of the greatest assets of the Christian is that his identity is rooted in the person of Jesus Christ.

———

DAY 80

Measuring Your Wealth

Scripture Reading: Romans 10:8–13   KEY Verse: Romans 10:13

Whoever calls on the name of the Lord shall be saved.

If someone asked you if you are wealthy, you might respond, "I pay my bills and have a little left over. I do better than some, but I am certainly not rich."

But did you know that in Christ Jesus you are immensely wealthy?

"I do not feel that blessed. From all indications, primarily my pocketbook, I definitely am not affluent."

You are using the wrong standard. The things that man honors, God despises. By God's measuring stick, you possess extraordinary riches. As a believer, you have the riches of God's grace bestowed upon you through the gift of His Son, Christ Jesus.

There is no circumstance, no problem, no obstacle that you face apart from the lavish grace of God. He gives wisdom, strength, guidance, patience, and love without limit. You are a wealthy saint because you have all the resources you need for life on earth, and in heaven, in the person of Jesus Christ.

God's help is available whenever you need it. Eternal life is yours forever. His undeserved blessings overflow into your heart daily.

You are a wealthy saint. The treasures of a new life in Christ are completely yours.

Goals for the Day

- Read Romans 10:8–13.
- Refer back to the verse of the day, Romans 10:13. Spend time praying for unsaved friends and loved ones.

Faith in Action

Is there someone you need to share the gospel with? What next steps do you need to take?

_____

_____

_____

_____

_____

_____

_____

_____

Master, thank You for bestowing Your riches on me. Thank You for the treasures of my new life in Christ. Eternal life. Blessings of wisdom, strength, guidance, and patience. Love without limit.

DAY 81

CLAIMING YOUR NEW POSITION

SCRIPTURE READING: Colossians 3:1–17   KEY VERSE: Colossians 3:3

You died, and your life is hidden with Christ in God.

Although financial poverty can occur through uncontrollable events, spiritual poverty is inexcusable for any born-again Christian.

Because we have been placed in Christ by God, we have constant, unlimited access to the Source of all spiritual blessings.

Why, then, do some walk well beneath the high calling of Scripture? Why do too many Christians suffer spiritual lack—living in perpetual defeat and disobedience?

The primary culprits that cause spiritual malnourishment are ignorance and unbelief. Our ignorance is of our astounding resources in Christ. We fail to realize we are no longer habitual sinners but justified saints.

But we must also believe. Unbelief will always keep Christians mired in spiritual poverty. As long as you think of yourself in nonbiblical terms, suffering from self-condemnation and self-pity, you will not experience the joy, peace, and power that come from faith in Jesus Christ. You are a wealthy saint. God has a high calling for you.

By faith and a scriptural confession of what God's Word says about you, claim your extravagant, new position in Christ.

Goals for the Day

- Read Colossians 3:1–17.
- Spend a few moments thinking about your spiritual identity in Christ. Ask God to help you deepen your awareness of everything you have in Jesus.

Faith in Action

Today's reading said, "By faith and a scriptural confession of what God's Word says about you, claim your extravagant, new position in Christ." Write down a few things that God's Word says about you.

_____

_____

_____

_____

_____

_____

_____

_____

Lord, on the basis of Your Word and by faith, I claim my new position in Christ. I am wealthy. You have a high and noble calling for me. I rejoice in my spiritual riches!

DAY 82

CHOSEN BY GOD

SCRIPTURE READING: 1 Peter 1:3–12   KEY VERSE: 1 Peter 1:3

Blessed be the God and Father of our Lord Jesus Christ, who according to His abundant mercy has begotten us again to a living hope through the resurrection of Jesus Christ from the dead.

Can you remember the rejection you felt when you were not chosen for the basketball team, the cheerleading squad, the college of your choice, or the promotion at work? Now, think of the thrill when you made the basketball team, were selected for the cheerleading squad, were accepted by the college you desired to attend, and received the promotion. You experienced great joy and gladness in being chosen.

Did you know that God chose you for salvation before the foundation of the world? Did you know that He was working out the miracle of your new birth in His mind before there was yet one evidence of creation?

Such undeserved love should stagger you, humble you, and drive you to profound adoration for the goodness, mercy, and grace of our Lord Jesus Christ.

God chose you. Think of the value that places on your life. It does not matter where you live, what you look like, what kind of car you drive, or your level of income.

Rejoice. You have been chosen by God and are forever His.

Goals for the Day

- Read 1 Peter 1:3–12.
- Review the key verse of the day, 1 Peter 1:3, and circle any words or phrases that stand out to you.

Faith in Action

Write down any new insights from today's reading.

_____

_____

_____

_____

_____

_____

_____

_____

_____

Dear heavenly Father, I often feel rejected by others. Thank You that You selected me for salvation before the foundation of the world. I am accepted. I am chosen. Thank You!

DAY 83

A Child of God

Scripture Reading: 1 Peter 1:13–21   Key Verse: Romans 9:23

*He might make known the riches of His
glory on the vessels of mercy, which He
had prepared beforehand for glory.*

All of us must individually receive God's offer of salvation (Eph. 1:13). Once we make a positive response of faith, the marvelous truth of God's sovereign working has just begun. We as believers are transformed for something far beyond our wildest imagination: "He predestined us to adoption as sons" (Eph. 1:5 NASB).

God did not save you just to escape the torment of hell and the condemnation of holy punishment. He saved you so that He might draw you into His household. You are a son or daughter of Yahweh God. As a child of God, you have the exhilarating prospect of fellowshipping intimately with your heavenly Father while depending on His loving provision. Forever, you will be a son or daughter of the Father.

You are also "predestined to become conformed to the image of His Son" (Rom. 8:29 NASB). The process of becoming like Christ begins at salvation. It continues through your life on earth. It will be consummated in heaven. God is at work irrevocably to make you like Himself. Can you think of anything more glorious?

Goals for the Day

- Read 1 Peter 1:13–21.
- Spend time in prayer giving thanks to God that "He predestined us to adoption as sons" (Eph. 1:5).

Faith in Action

Today's reading said, "You are a son or daughter of Yahweh God." Write down what that truth means to you.

_____

_____

_____

_____

_____

_____

_____

_____

_____

Almighty God, please continue to conform me to the image of Your Son. I praise You that You are at work irrevocably in my life.

DAY 84

Heir to an Immeasurable Fortune

Scripture Reading: Psalm 19   KEY Verse: Acts 20:32

*So now, brethren, I commend you to God and to the word
of His grace, which is able to build you up and give you
an inheritance among all those who are sanctified.*

"If only I were rich or famous my future would be secure." Most of us have probably dreamed what our lives would be like if we were heirs to massive fortunes.

How would your thinking and living change if today you understood that you are the heir of treasures beside which even the wealthiest earthly estates pale?

The amazing truth is that God has named you an heir of His holdings: "And now I commend you to God and to the word of His grace, which is able . . . to give you the inheritance among all those who are sanctified" (Acts 20:32 NASB).

What does He own? He owns it all. As Creator of heaven and earth and all that is in them, God is the sole proprietor of the universe. It is in His hands to bestow His unspeakable wealth upon you.

God is your Father. You are His son or daughter. All that is His belongs to you. And all that you have comes from Him. You have an inheritance that will never fade or tarnish because you are an heir of the Father's immeasurable fortune.

Goals for the Day

- Read Psalm 19.
- Use Psalm 19 to guide your prayer time. Choose specific verses that prompt you to praise God.

Faith in Action

Today's reading asked, "How would your thinking and living change if today you understood that you are the heir of treasures beside which even the wealthiest earthly estates pale?" Write your thoughts below.

_____

_____

_____

_____

_____

_____

_____

O God, You are my Father. I am Your child. All You have belongs to me. Thank You for an inheritance that will never fade.

DAY 85

Eternal Life

Scripture Reading: Psalm 103   Key Verse: Psalm 103:4

Who redeems your life from destruction, who crowns you with lovingkindness and tender mercies.

Whether on the streets of Mumbai or in a plush oceanfront home, whether clothed in tattered jeans or a fine suit, you can enjoy the good life that Jesus Christ imparts to all who believe and abide in Him. The good life is eternal life received as a gift through faith in Christ's sacrifice for our sins.

Eternal life is as good as it gets. It is the everlasting, unending, unceasing presence of the eternal God, lavishing all of His goodness upon you in His limitless mercy and grace. It is a permanent possession, unaffected by the rise and fall of money, people, or nations. It is guaranteed by Christ's death, burial, and resurrection.

But you can experience the reality of eternal life here and now. A new quality of life is available to all who have become one with the Savior. It is the abundant sufficiency of Christ for every circumstance.

Each day is an opportunity to draw from the divine well of peace, joy, love, faithfulness, gentleness, goodness, patience, and self-control without diminishing the supply by one ounce. Do not ever be deceived. Real life is in Jesus, and Jesus is in you. Inexhaustible, boundless life for you forever.

Goals for the Day

- Read John 17.
- Write down any key verses in John 17 that stood out to you.

Faith in Action

What does John 17 tell you about experiencing the reality of eternal life here and now? How should that make a difference in how you live every day?

_____

_____

_____

_____

_____

_____

_____

Precious heavenly Father, thank You for the inexhaustible, boundless life that is in Your Son, Jesus. Let me continually draw from Your divine resources.

DAY 86

ABUNDANT LIFE

SCRIPTURE READING: Isaiah 43   KEY Verses: Isaiah 43:18–19

Do not remember the former things, nor consider the things of old. Behold, I will do a new thing, now it shall spring forth; shall you not know it? I will even make a road in the wilderness and rivers in the desert.

In *The Root of the Righteous,* A. W. Tozer urged readers, "Keep your feet on the ground, but let your heart soar as high as it will. Refuse to be average or to surrender to the chill of your spiritual environment."[1]

As believers, we must live out the truth given to us in Hebrews 11. Our citizenship is registered in heaven where we have an eternal destiny. When we view life with this perspective, our outlook is positive and hope filled.

We are fully alive through Jesus Christ, who lives in us by the power of His Spirit. In fact, we are much more alive now that we have received God's Son as our Savior than when we walked this earth in physical form only. We are alive eternally to spiritual things that were once beyond our ability to understand.

The Old Testament saints could only imagine what was to come. They lived and died in their faith. However, they were not disappointed. Their devotion to God—and His to them—was sufficient for all their needs (Dan. 12:2; Heb. 11:13–16).

Are you living as Tozer suggested, keeping your feet firmly planted in the truth of God's Word, all the while dreaming and thinking of what God has for you in the not-so-distant future? Jesus came so that we might have abundant life now—a tiny foretaste of what is yet to be.

Goals for the Day

- Read Isaiah 43.
- Spend a few moments thinking about what new things God is bringing to pass for you and let that guide your prayer time.

Faith in Action

Glance back at the Tozer quote from today's reading. What resonates with you about his words? Write your thoughts below.

_____

_____

_____

_____

_____

Almighty God, I want to keep my feet on the ground while my heart soars to heights unlimited. Help me not to surrender to the chill of my spiritual environment. Plant my feet firmly in Your Word as I dream of the unlimited future You have planned for me.

DAY 87

Contentment

Scripture Reading: Philippians 4:6–13   Key Verse: Philippians 4:12

I know how to be abased, and I know how to abound. Everywhere and in all things I have learned both to be full and to be hungry, both to abound and to suffer need.

We struggle enough over the issue of contentment, and most of us live in fairly good conditions with enough to eat and clothes to wear. Imagine Paul in prison, without some of the basic necessities and without personal freedom, and read his words carefully: "Not that I speak from want, for I have learned to be content in whatever circumstances I am. I know how to get along with humble means, and I also know how to live in prosperity; in any and every circumstance I have learned the secret of being filled and going hungry, both of having abundance and suffering need. I can do all things through Him who strengthens me" (Phil. 4:11–13 NASB).

Paul was not a blind and foolhardy optimist who denied reality. He had already endured much physical hardship, yet he could still look at his bleak prospects, humanly speaking, and say he was truly content. When he said that Christ was his strength for everything, he meant *everything*. He did not try to count his "haves" and "have-nots" in a spirit of worry or fear. Paul knew that God's best for him was found by abiding in Christ daily, trusting Him to furnish what he needed.

Goals for the Day

- Read Philippians 4:6–13.
- Let Paul's words from today's Bible reading guide your prayer time.

Faith in Action

Write down any new insights that stood out to you from today's reading.

___

Thank You, God, for what You have graciously given me: food, shelter, friends, and family. I trust You to furnish any lack in my life. Teach me to be content.

DAY 88

Complete in Christ

Scripture Reading: Colossians 2:6–10   Key Verse: Colossians 2:10

*You are complete in Him, who is the head
of all principality and power.*

On a scale of one to ten, how complete would you say your life is? What person, job, object, or achievement would make your life more fulfilling? Most of us would have probably scored moderately high on the first question and added a few names or items to the second.

Did you know, though, that the apostle Paul insisted that once we place our trust in Christ as Savior, at that instant we become "complete in Him"? The word *complete* in the original Greek meant "full." When a person is full, he has no room for anything more. Think about this: If Christ is in you, your life is a "ten." In Jesus Christ is "the fullness of Deity" (Col. 2:9 NASB). That is, Christ is the sum of all perfection—without blemish or want.

That same Christ resides in you and supplies all your needs. Therefore, when you have Christ, you have it all. You lack nothing. You possess eternal and abundant life. In Him are all of the wisdom, love, patience, kindness, and comfort you will ever need. No demand is unmet through the limitless resources of the indwelling Christ. Since you are complete in Him, your search for meaning is over. Christ is your life, and that is enough.

Goals for the Day

- Read Colossians 2:6–10.
- Write down the key verse of the day, Colossians 2:10, on a notecard or on your phone. Over the next several days, commit the verse to memory.

Faith in Action

Write down your thoughts on what it means to be "complete in Christ."

_____

_____

_____

_____

_____

_____

_____

_____

_____

_____

Almighty Lord, thank You that I am complete in You. My life is a "ten." All my needs are supplied. I have it all. I lack nothing!

DAY 89

Your Future Reward

Scripture Reading: 1 Corinthians 3:1–14   Key Verse: Revelation 22:12

Behold, I am coming quickly, and My reward is with Me, to give to every one according to his work.

When the sixteenth-century Polish astronomer Nicolas Copernicus first proposed that the earth revolves around the sun, not vice versa, he was met with scorn and ridicule. It was years later that his theory was found to be entirely accurate. Life often seems that way. Ignorant men are treated as kings, while the wise are ignored.

Even worse, sometimes the evil are exalted, while the godly are afflicted. The psalmist contemplated this seeming injustice in Psalm 73: "Behold, these are the wicked; and always at ease, they have increased in wealth. Surely in vain I have kept my heart pure" (vv. 12–13 NASB).

In the Sermon on the Mount, Jesus indicated that His followers would be persecuted on earth. He went on to say, however, that they should rejoice in such treatment because their "reward in heaven is great" (Matt. 5:12 NASB).

Believers are justly recompensed in heaven for their conduct on earth—as they trust the Lord to do His works through them. All inequities and injustices are more than compensated by the rewards that Christ will distribute to His followers.

Whether or not you are now recognized at work or home, whether or not you are treated with due respect, remember that God will honor your obedience for all eternity.

Goals for the Day

- Read 1 Corinthians 3:1–14.
- Write down anything that stood out to you in today's reading.

Faith in Action

Spend some time thinking about the verse of the day, Revelation 22:12. How does this verse impact the way you want to live?

_____

_____

_____

_____

_____

_____

_____

Dear heavenly Father, I rejoice in the knowledge that all inequities and injustices will be compensated in eternity. Until that time, help me continue to do Your work Your way.

DAY 90

YOU HAVE IT ALL

SCRIPTURE READING: John 1:1–18   KEY VERSE: John 1:4

In Him was life, and the life was the light of men.

Every individual who has trusted Jesus for his salvation has received the Source for his most compelling needs in the person of the indwelling Christ.

Christ is the Bread of Life. He is the Sustenance who nourishes our innermost being. Our hunger for meaning and purpose in life is fully satisfied in Christ. He is our fulfillment; He is our identity. We want not for significance when we have Christ as our life.

Christ is the Water of Life. He channels His all-sufficient life through our earthen vessels—drenching us with His joy, peace, love, hope, contentment, strength, and steadfastness. He quenches our thirst for self-worth, assuring us of our inestimable value to Him. He freely gives us His abundant life.

Christ is the Light of Life. He enlightens us with eternal truth, bequeathing us wisdom for the journey. He sheds His light upon what is truly valuable so that we can pursue the things that are profitable, not foolishly chasing empty dreams or false, deceiving philosophies.

When you have Christ, you have it all—meaning, purpose, life in its fullest sense, truth, and wisdom. You belong to the Creator, Sustainer, and End of all things.

Goals for the Day

- Read John 1:1–18.
- Use John's words from John 1:1–18 to guide your prayer and worship time.

Faith in Action

Jesus has everything you need to live a life of passion, purpose, and peace. Write down any key insights you've learned and next steps to take in your walk with Christ.

_____

_____

_____

_____

_____

_____

_____

Jesus, You are my Bread of Life. You are my Sustenance. You are the Water of Life, channeling Your sufficiency through me. You are the Light of Life, giving wisdom for the journey ahead. In You, dear Lord, I have it all!

Endnotes

Days 1–10
1. Hannah Whitall Smith, *The Christian's Secret of a Happy Life* (F. H. Revell, 1888), 63–64.

Days 11–20
1. Penelope J. Stokes, *Faith: The Substance of Things Unseen* (Carol Stream, IL: Tyndale House Publishers, 1996), 109–113.
2. Earl O. Roe, *Dream Big: The Henrietta Mears Story* (Tyndale House, 2016).

Days 21–40
1. Neil Anderson, *Who I Am in Christ: A Devotional* (Baker Publishing, 2001), 40–41.

Days 41–50
1. Peter Marshall, *Mr. Jones, Meet the Master: Sermons and Prayers of Peter Marshall* (F. H. Revell, 1952), 145.
2. Dwight L. Moody, *The Overcoming Life and Other Sermons* (New York,: Fleming H. Revell Co., 1896), 28–29.
3. Martin H. Manser, *The Westminster Collection of Christian Quotations* (Louisville, KY: Westminster John Knox Press, 2001), 332.
4. Adam Clarke, *Adam Clarke's Commentary on the Bible* (Grand Rapids, MI: Baker Book House, 1985), 23.

Endnotes

Days 51–60

1. F. B. Meyer, *Through the Bible Day by Day: A Devotional Commentary* (Philadelphia, PA: The American Sunday School Union, 1914), 22–23.
2. W. E. Vines, *Vine's Expository Dictionary of New Testament Words* (Reformed Church Publications, 2015), 92.

Days 61–70

1. Dr. and Mrs. Howard Taylor, *Hudson Taylor and the China Inland Mission* (London, UK: The Religious Tract Society, 1921), 169.
2. "Chamberlain and Hitler 1938," The National Archives, accessed June 12, 2025, https://www.nationalarchives.gov.uk/education/resources/chamberlain-and-hitler/.

Days 71–80

1. J. D. Douglas et al., eds., *The New Bible Dictionary*, 2nd ed. (Wheaton, IL: Tyndale House Publishers, 1982), 990.

Days 81–90

1. A. W. Tozer, *The Root of the Righteous* (Moody, 2015), 15.

About the Author

Dr. Charles F. Stanley was the founder of In Touch Ministries and Pastor Emeritus of First Baptist Church of Atlanta, Georgia, where he served more than 50 years. He was also a *New York Times* bestselling author of more than seventy books. Until his death in 2023, Dr. Stanley's mission was to get the gospel to "as many people as possible, as quickly as possible, as clearly as possible, as irresistibly as possible, through the power of the Holy Spirit to the glory of God." This is a calling In Touch Ministries continues to pursue by transmitting his teachings as widely and effectively as possible.

Dr. Stanley's messages can be heard daily on "In Touch with Dr. Charles Stanley" broadcasts on television, radio, and satellite networks and stations around the world; on the Internet at intouch.org and through In Touch+ and the Charles Stanley Institute; and via the In Touch Messenger Lab. Dr. Stanley's inspiring messages are also published in the award-winning *In Touch* devotional magazine.

The perfect campus for your calling.

CHARLES STANLEY
INSTITUTE

Based on our founder's 50-plus years of biblical teachings, the online campus of Charles Stanley Institute will equip you for stronger faith and deeper discipleship. Enroll now and unlock your full potential for kingdom impact!

charlesstanleyinstitute.org